Simone de Beauvoir

Les Belles Images

La Femme rompue

Terry Keefe

Professor of French Studies
University of Lancaster

UNIVERSITY OF GLASGOW
FRENCH AND GERMAN PUBLICATIONS
2005

University of Glasgow French and German Publications

Series Editors: Mark G. Ward (German)
Geoff Woollen (French)

Modern Languages Building, University of Glasgow,
Glasgow G12 8QL, Scotland.

First published 1991. Reprinted 1998 and 2005.

Printed by Juma Printing and Publishing, Sheffield S1 4HD.

ISBN 0 85261 269 9

Contents

References

The bracketed references in **bold** typeface found in the respective chapters are to the current Gallimard 'Folio' editions of *Les Belles Images* (no. 243) and *La Femme rompue* (no. 960).

To avoid ambiguity between the story and the collection bearing its name, quotation marks are used to designate the part ('La Femme rompue') of the whole (*La Femme rompue*). For the sake of uniformity they apply also to 'L'Âge de discrétion' and 'Monologue'.

Bracketed references marked *TCF* are to the Gallimard 'Folio' edition of *Tout compte fait* (no. 1022), and those marked *PI* are to Beauvoir's *prière d'insérer* for *La Femme rompue,* reprinted in Francis and Gontier (1979), pp. 231-2.

Full details of works by Beauvoir and others that are referred to in summary fashion in the footnotes to each chapter will be found in the Select Bibliography.

Introduction

One of the obvious reasons for examining Simone de Beauvoir's last two works of fiction together, as well as certain similarities in their subject matter, is that they were written and published over a period of scarcely more than two years. *Les Belles Images,* which she began in the autumn of 1965, came out in November 1966; and her collection of three stories, *La Femme rompue,* appeared in book form at the beginning of 1968. In order to set these books in their appropriate context, therefore, one needs to consider the position that Beauvoir had reached by the middle of the 1960s in her career as a writer and in the development of her ideas.

Born in 1908, she began to break free from her conventional and stifling upbringing in a bourgeois family in Paris only when she became a student at the Sorbonne. In 1929 she embarked on the famous relationship with her fellow student, Jean-Paul Sartre, that was to last until Sartre's death in 1980. It was not until 1943 that she published her first book, the novel *L'Invitée,* but soon after this the French intellectual scene came to be dominated by existentialism, the philosophical trend of which Sartre and Beauvoir were seen as the leading exponents. The mid to late 1940s constituted a particularly productive phase of Beauvoir's career as a writer: she published two more novels (*Le Sang des autres* and *Tous les hommes sont mortels*); one play; an account of her travels in America; five philosophical essays; and in 1949 her best-known work, the two-volume study of women, *Le Deuxième Sexe.* Her lengthy novel relating the fortunes of left-wing intellectuals in Paris in the immediate postwar years, *Les Mandarins,* won the prestigious Prix Goncourt in 1954, but her major literary project in the ensuing years was the writing of her memoirs, the four volumes of which appeared in 1958, 1960, 1963 and 1972. In 1979, Gallimard brought out for the first time a collection of stories, *Quand prime le spirituel,* that Beauvoir had written but left aside in the 1930s, thereby completing the range of her published fiction with the first stories that she finished; the collection is similar in certain respects to her very last stories, *La Femme rompue.* Between 1968 and her death in 1986, Beauvoir turned to other forms of writing and activity.

Emphasis on Beauvoir's career as a novelist gives few clues about her philosophical evolution or those aspects of her personal life that impinged upon her writings. The relevance of the latter, however, is far greater for some of her published works than for others. Having produced extensive autobiographical material in the twelve-year gap between *Les Mandarins* and *Les Belles Images,* Beauvoir had little need to transpose her life into fiction by the mid-1960s. The impulse to write what became her two final books of fiction sprang not from private concerns or preoccupations, but from what she saw in the world around her. Hence the incentive to trace back features of these stories to Beauvoir's own life is minimal, as is the temptation to identify any of the central women figures with the author herself. Indeed, the fact that there are far fewer obvious connections between her personal life and these two books than in the case of her earlier creative works is doubtless one reason why some reviewers regarded them as atypical of Beauvoir's writings, and saw them as expressing views that she indignantly denied were her own.

The question of the extent to which *Les Belles Images* and *La Femme rompue* specifically reflect a later stage in the development of Beauvoir's philosophical and sociopolitical ideas is worth much closer attention. Her early espousal of the existentialist framework that Sartre expounded in great technical detail in *L'Être et le Néant* (1943) was quite explicit, and can best be illustrated by reference to two of her published works. The essay *Pour une morale de l'ambiguïté* (1947) was an undisguised attempt to demonstrate that it was possible to base a positive morality upon the metaphysics of *L'Être et le Néant,* provided that one accepted responsibility for one's existence and acted in the name of freedom. And two years later Beauvoir made it clear in the introduction to *Le Deuxième Sexe* that her analysis of women's position in the world was based upon the same philosophical beliefs. What gave this book its impact were her ideas that women have no specific nature of their own, only a particular 'situation' in the world; and that 'femininity' is no more than a socially constructed myth to which men encourage women to conform. But at the very heart of her argument was the assertion that all human beings are free. If men are to blame for trying to impose particular patterns of behaviour upon women, women themselves are morally at fault insofar as they consent to, and comply with, those patterns. Certain differences of emphasis are detectable between Sartre and Beauvoir, who also developed lines of his reasoning in directions that he himself did not pursue. But there is no doubt that throughout the 1930s and 1940s their considered perspectives on life were virtually identical and that, philosophically speaking, Beauvoir saw herself as following Sartre's lead. However, when Sartre came to consider himself in some sense a Marxist in the early 1950s—by 1959 declaring that Marxism is the 'unsurpassable' philosophy for the twentieth century and existentialism no more than an ideology within it—Beauvoir was at first reluctant to follow him. They continued, nevertheless, to be committed to exactly the same social and political causes, and Beauvoir's *Privilèges* (1955) and *La Longue Marche* (1957) are essays exactly in tune with Sartre's new thinking. Some will wish to see such apparent agreement as just a public façade that Beauvoir had deep psychological reasons for wishing to maintain, but however this may be, one can still discern obvious divergences in the patterns of their published works after 1949. The very success of *Le Deuxième Sexe* made it inevitable that Beauvoir should write increasingly about, and from the point of view of, women, and Sartre's ever-growing preoccupation with political issues can now be seen to provide a certain explanation of why he should have published no more fiction at all after 1949.

In short, whilst it is essential to bear in mind both Beauvoir's existentialist beginnings and the general Marxist orientation of her thought from the mid-1950s onwards, there is much less reason than there would have been in connection with earlier periods to expect Sartre's theoretical positions at the time to shed detailed light on *Les Belles Images* and *La Femme rompue*. It is Beauvoir's own particular ideas, concerns and emphases that give these two books their most distinctive features and draw together all of the works that she produced between 1958 and 1968.

The first volume of Beauvoir's memoirs, *Mémoires d'une jeune fille rangée* (1958), looks back in the obvious sense that it recounts the first twenty-one years or so of her life. But it also looks forward, partly because it prepares the way for the second volume, *La Force de l'âge* (1960), by naturally raising the question of what became of the girl described in the first; and partly because it ushers in a preoccupation with the importance of childhood and upbringing that will be with Beauvoir for the rest of her career. She came to believe that the central postulate of *Le Deuxième Sexe,* 'On ne naît pas femme: on le devient', needed to be supplemented by the parallel axiom 'On ne naît pas mâle, on le devient' (*TCF,* 614), since the circumstances and quality of childhood are crucial to the development of both sexes. Hence *Les Belles Images* and each of the stories in *La Femme rompue* take up the theme of upbringing; and at least two of them pursue the further point that every parent is in some measure the product of her or his own childhood.

In this last respect, an important element of the context in which Beauvoir's two final works of fiction need to be set is the published work that immediately preceded them, *Une mort très douce* (1964). In this brief but fascinating account of roughly the last month of her mother's life, Beauvoir is clearly recording a major re-evaluation of her view of her mother and of the relationship between them. Inescapably, this involves thinking about the strict upbringing that she and her sister underwent. But it also logically leads Beauvoir to explain this in turn (and, to some extent, excuse it) by reference to her mother's own childhood. There are already signs in *Une mort très douce* that these processes of thought had a marked effect upon Beauvoir, so that it is hardly surprising that the same patterns of analysis should find their way into stories written shortly afterwards. This is by no means to suggest a simple and direct 'causal' link between Beauvoir's life and these later stories. The themes of childhood and relations with one's mother were present in novels like *Le Sang des autres* and *Les Mandarins,* which she wrote many years before her mother's death. In any case, *Les Belles Images* and *La Femme rompue,* as already noted, are not autobiographical in any useful sense of the term, and this fact seems to have resulted from a conscious decision taken by Beauvoir after the publication of *Une mort très douce:* 'Ce livre avait encore un caractère auto-biographique. Quand je l'eus achevé, je me suis promis de ne plus parler de moi d'ici longtemps'(*TCF,* 169). Part of the interest of these two works of fiction lies in the particular kind of distance that Beauvoir puts between herself and topics that may have been preoccupying her personally in the mid-1960s.

In seeking to understand her general state of mind at that time, one might regard the notorious epilogue to the third volume of her memoirs, *La Force des choses* (completed and published in 1963), as the obvious starting point. But Beauvoir was soon to explain that the despair apparently expressed in that ending—'je mesure avec stupeur à quel point j'ai été flouée'—had been much misunderstood (partly as a result of her own 'maladresse littéraire'), since it related as much to the horrors of the Algerian War as to ageing and other private circumstances.[1] Personal problems and concerns, in fact, never diverted Beauvoir's attention for very long from the world around her, and even the Algerian War was only one aspect—albeit a catastrophic one—of what she regarded as a whole chain of deplorable events and developments in postwar France. She looked upon the economic recovery of the 1950s and 1960s with no favour at all, since she saw it as associated with the growth of a capitalist, consumer society based ultimately upon oppression. The place of women in such a society continued to be a secondary one, and the optimism about women's emancipation that she had expressed in *Le*

---

[1] Interview in Jeanson, pp. 269-75.

Deuxième Sexe looked increasingly misplaced. And, perhaps above all, in the mid-1960s Beauvoir saw all the iniquities of the French social and political system being covered up and hidden in a wave of spurious optimism about the future:

> Moi je ne vois pas pourquoi, sous prétexte qu'on fait confiance à l'avenir, qu'on croit qu'un jour il y aura une société socialiste, on devrait taire la part d'échec et de malheur que comporte toute vie. Ou alors je trouve que l'optimisme socialiste ressemble beaucoup à l'optimisme technocratique qui sévit aujourd'hui, qui appelle la misère abondance et qui se sert de l'avenir comme d'un alibi.[2]

Having often defended the desirability of recording failure, injustice and suffering in both the private and public domains, Beauvoir again set out, in 1965-1967, to do just this in what were to be her last two fictional works.

---

[2] In Buin, p. 91.

Chapter One

Les Belles Images

Beauvoir relates, in *Tout compte fait,* that in the autumn of 1965 she abandoned the project of completing a novel about ageing, and set about writing *Les Belles Images.* An interview given at the beginning of November makes it clear that, if she did not have a precise subject in mind by that stage, her main concern was already to distance herself from her characters in a way that would require new narrative techniques:

> Si j'écris un autre roman, il est bien certain qu'il ne sera pas du même genre, et qu'il me posera des problèmes techniques nouveaux (manière de raconter, distance par rapport aux personnages, etc.); en outre, il s'agira de gens qui ne seront pas du tout placés dans les mêmes situations que moi.[1]

Les Belles Images was written quickly, being finished early in 1966 and published in November. A bestseller for some three months, it received a mixed reception at the hands of reviewers, some of whom had difficulty in understanding why Beauvoir had apparently left behind the obvious moral and political concerns of her earlier fiction to enter the glittering world of the contemporary jet set.

Society

Although *Les Belles Images* centres on Laurence and her problems, Beauvoir's own account of her intentions in writing it lays greater emphasis on her wish to depict a particular society: 'J'ai repris un autre projet: évoquer cette société technocratique dont je me tiens le plus possible à distance mais dans laquelle néanmoins je vis' (*TCF,* 172). And the story does, indeed, conjure up vividly the way of life, the values, and the language of at least a certain stratum of French society in the mid-1960s, when modernization and technical progress were the keynotes of the process of development. More precisely, while focusing sharply upon a group of people

---

[1] Interview in Jeanson, p. 295. Interestingly, the origin of Beauvoir's first published novel, *L'Invitée,* was a suggestion by Sartre that she should begin putting more of herself directly into her stories!

representing this particular stratum or class, the book simultaneously assigns them a place in relation to their society and even the world as a whole. For it is of the very essence of the work not to show the 'grosse bourgeoisie technocratique' in complete isolation, but to indicate in a variety of ways, some implicit and oblique, that this is only one very specific part of French society. Equally, French society itself is seen to belong to the category of Western capitalist societies, and is contrasted with countries that are technologically and economically less advanced. These aspects of the novel constitute the indispensable context for the central character's dramas or dilemmas and they need to be examined in detail before the character of Laurence herself can be fully analysed.

In reading the book we form our impressions of the class that Beauvoir is depicting in at least three major, interrelated ways: by reacting to particular characters as individuals; by observing how such characters behave when gathered together; and by 'listening' to, and evaluating, their explicit justifications of their way of life.

Three main social occasions figure in the book. Weekend gatherings at Feuverolles, the mansion outside Paris owned by Laurence's mother, Dominique, are described in chapter I and again early in chapter III; and a New Year's Eve dinner party at the home of Marthe, Laurence's sister, forms the end-piece to chapter III. (There is an echo of this last occasion in the final chapter, in the form of a dinner party at Dominique's flat, but this is a 'réunion de famille' and has a different purpose.) The first of these, placed as it is at the very beginning of the book (**7-18**), has an especially strong effect upon the reader, but leaves somewhat confused impressions, because we are projected very abruptly into a milieu different from our own. The second, in the very middle of the book (**87-101**), runs parallel to the first in many respects, but serves to reinforce and refine most of the impressions initially conveyed. The third (**141-52**) takes this process still further (by now we are sickened by the class of people on display), before proposing a possible 'escape' from the milieu concerned, when Laurence is given the long-awaited opportunity of a holiday alone with her father. Chapter IV, of course, is entirely dominated by this trip to Greece and its aftermath: it does eventually take Laurence to the point where a partial break with some aspects of technocratic society may be effected, but after chapter III Beauvoir has no further need to illustrate in detail what that society involves.

What does it involve, then, and in what ways do the behaviour and comments of its members in company seem so objectionable to readers? An obsession with money is probably the first point to strike us, and it is the particular obsession of those who already have more than enough and wish to flaunt the fact ('«je n'en suis pas à un million près», a dit Gilbert'—**7**). But in various forms the theme of money runs through all of the first three chapters (falling away, like certain other elements, in chapter IV). Money counts far less for Laurence than for those around her, and she is genuinely horrified to discover, for instance, that Jean-Charles's main reaction to the accident with the cyclist is concern about the financial loss sustained. She speculates gloomily about the results of a test that she would like the members of her social circle to take: 'Qui choisirait sincèrement de payer huit cent mille francs pour sauver la vie d'un inconnu?' (**150**).

Yet, even for the jet set of *Les Belles Images,* money is primarily important for what it can buy, and this not only in the narrow sense of physical objects and possessions, for they clearly believe that it buys, or is somehow closely associated with, social status ('«il y avait là tous les gens qui comptent à Paris»'—**92-93**). Consequently, they are prepared to exclude certain people from their gatherings, when appropriate: 'il est devenu l'avocat le plus célèbre de France. Du coup Marthe et Hubert n'ont pas été invités. Ils présentent mal' (**87**). Indeed, their social snobbery and ambition is such that they are inevitably in competition with one another in some measure. This often gives an unpleasant edge to their social intercourse ('Pourquoi prennent-ils tant de plaisir à se mettre en pièces les uns les autres?'— **9**), but in any case it alienates the reader, as well as Laurence, because of the conspicuous excesses involved, whether these relate to expensive meals (**92**) and holidays (**9-10**; **90-91**), or to the deliberately useless New Year gifts that they vie with each other to find (**145**). It is clear, furthermore, that, for all their money and status, the technocrats are far from happy and content: rather, in a variety of ways, they are victims of their own success.

Above all, however, the novel suggests—largely through the sensitivity of Laurence—that the affluent way of life of the class represented is maintained at the expense of those who are less privileged. Just as Laurence is surprised to learn of the relative poverty of the workers of Brasilia (**11**), so she is shocked to hear that most of the new council flats being built still have no bathroom, although she is silenced by the argument that profits have to be made if any flats are to be built at all (**148-9**). The attitudes of her left-wing colleague Mona also make her aware of how privileged her own existence is, and the image of young working girls that disturbs Catherine's friend Brigitte ('«toute la journée elles mettent des ronds de carotte sur des filets de hareng»'—**79**) finally affects Laurence too. Her attempts to persuade herself with the standard justifications— 'c'est qu'elles ne sont pas capables d'un travail plus intéressant' (**80**)—are unsuccessful. In short, although Laurence's attitude towards 'la condition ouvrière' is an ambiguous one (**73**), she does at least show some concern about it from time to time and is not prepared to accept the 'official' explanation that a successful society necessarily involves some (doubtless regrettable) casualties, in the form of individual misfortune or misery ('faux frais'; 'incidences humaines'—**58; 80**). The same pattern applies on the global scale. Again, Laurence is moved by the poster that haunts Catherine ('Pouvoir de l'image. «Les deux tiers du monde ont faim», et cette tête d'enfant'—**29**). And again she tries in vain to explain it away in a facile manner. Moreover, while her discovery of the poverty in Greece and her concern for the dismal future of the little girl in the café (**158**) are set firmly in a personal context, the net effect is still to show that Laurence is a great deal less indifferent to human suffering than the social set to which she belongs.

This is why the bitter argument with Jean-Charles, in which he charges her with over-sensitivity ('sensiblerie') and talks scathingly about her 'mauvaise conscience' (**133-4**), is so crucial. Laurence may have little idea about how to change the world, or even French society, but she acknowledges that all is not well. Although the rich bourgeois surrounding her also know this, they are not prepared to admit it. They continue to go their own wealthy way unperturbed, and worse, they invent 'rational' justifications for doing so. It is these justifications that Beauvoir was so anxious to ridicule in *Les Belles Images*. All of the key arguments of the technocrats concerning the current state of the world involve the assertion that things will be better in the future. Thus even the poster depicting a starving child can be interpreted in optimistic fashion: 'Cette affiche prouve que nous voulons que les choses changent. Maintenant on peut produire beaucoup plus de nourriture qu'avant, et les transporter vite et facilement des pays riches aux pays pauvres' (**30**). Laurence notices, for example, that all of the books that Jean-Charles has lent her tell the same story: 'tout va beaucoup mieux qu'avant, tout ira mieux plus tard. [...] on peut considérer que vers 1990 sera instaurée la civilisation de l'abondance et des loisirs' (**72-73**). In twenty years, it is claimed, France will have solved all of its problems: 'Triomphe de l'urbanisme: partout des cités radieuses qui ressemblent, sur cent vingt mètres de hauteur, à des ruches, à des fourmilières, mais ruisselantes de soleil' (**148**). The very idea of man and human nature will be changed (**94**). This is transparent nonsense, and not only because we are now in a position to evaluate the predictions about 1990. Yet however little plausibility or coherence these ideas may have, they are ideas that enjoyed great popularity when Beauvoir was writing. She took them all, together with other clichés used by her characters, from books, newspapers, and magazines of the mid-1960s. Her fundamental objection to such views is less that they incorporate unlikely visions of the future, than that they constitute a way of trying to cover up the realities of the present. It is the technocratic bourgeoisie itself that enjoys all the advantages of technological progress. In order to continue doing so its members need to hide from others, and to try to hide from themselves, its cost in human terms. The simple fact is that serious poverty and suffering, in France and elsewhere, underlie their own privileged state:

> La presse, la télévision, la publicité, la mode, lancent des slogans, des mythes, que les gens intériorisent et qui leur masquent le monde réel. Prenez le mythe de l'avenir, qui m'irrite particulièrement: une maniére d'éviter de voir le présent. La 'France de demain', titre d'une émission diffusée en 1965, on nous en rebat les oreilles pour nous cacher celle d'aujourd'hui, où règne ni la civilisation des loisirs ni celle de l'abondance. C'est immoral et déshonnête.[2]

Characters

There are a number of lesser characters in *Les Belles Images* who have little, if any, function other than that of representing the class that Beauvoir is attacking. Illustrating graphically the assumptions and values she is ridiculing, they appear only in those sections of the book where social gatherings are depicted. The Thirion couple, for instance, are present only at the second weekend session at Feuverolles. Mme Thirion ('une idiote patentée'—**95**) throws absurdly ostentatious and banal elements into the conversation (**90**; **97**); and Thirion himself, one of the most famous lawyers in France ('«cette crapule»'—**105**), holds forth pretentiously on the indispensability of lawyers (**94**), his own cases, and how women will never achieve as much in the profession as men (**99**). The Dufrène couple are at each of the social gatherings in the book. Dufrène, a colleague and friend of Jean-Charles, is equally preoccupied with money, but also has the same blind confidence in new technology and

---

[2] Interview with Jacqueline Piatier (in Stefanson, p. 56).

the future. Just as Dufrène believes the architecture of Brasilia to be
'«dépassé»' (11), so his wife considers feminism '«dépassé»' (99).
She finds most things 'merveilleux' and makes the same kind of
comments as Mme Thirion. The unpleasantness towards others that
we see her to be capable of from the beginning (9) is rather echoed
by the competitive edge to her husband's relationship with Jean-
Charles. And the fact that she needs sleeping pills and other drugs is
made to suggest that she, like others in this social circle, experiences
inner tensions ('ils ne consommeraient pas tant de tranquillisants, de
décontrariants s'ils étaient contents'—83). By reference to the
Dufrènes, the Thirions and a host of other characters who appear
briefly or are regularly mentioned by name, we build up a detailed
picture of the people with whom Laurence mixes socially, or at least
of the way in which she sees them.

Another cluster of characters more intimately bound up with the
main story of the novel also serve first and foremost to instantiate
the class that Beauvoir is castigating. Laurence does not actually
meet, in the course of the book, Gilbert Mortier's ex-wife, Marie-
Claire, or his ex-mistress, Lucile de Saint-Chaumont, but the very
fact that Marie-Claire sides with the latter simply out of hatred for
Dominique says a great deal about her. And when Lucile's daughter
Patricia is first mentioned, Laurence's reaction is revealing: 'Elle a
vu une fois Patricia, une fillette de douze ans, blonde et maniérée; et
sa photo l'année dernière, tout en blanc au bal des debs; une
ravissante dinde, fauchée, que sa mère jette dans des bras riches'
(46-47). Gilbert himself, at fifty-six, is one of the richest men in
France. With his wealth, his power, and his faith in capitalism, he
represents the values of the French technocrats more starkly than any
other character. Despite Laurence's hostility, his decision to break
with Dominique is hardly, in itself, an especially blameworthy one,
and until she reacts in a particularly odious way he appears to be
trying to deal with the matter fairly decently. Yet he is, in general, a
very hard man, whose claim that we are passing into a period when
'«les hommes deviendront inutiles»' (94) is entirely consistent with
his lack of concern about the fate of individuals. Although Laurence
finds it obscene that the word 'aimer' should pass his lips, some of
his phrases expressing his view of the world echo in her head and she
even considers that some of his ideas may be right (177). When
Dominique crosses Gilbert, however, he becomes physically violent,
certainly manhandling her, and possibly even assaulting her sexually
(124). He disappears from the story at this point, but has already
made a powerful impact, largely, no doubt, because he has become a

kind of nightmare figure for Laurence and a threat to her fragile stability.

For not all of the characters who have significant dealings with Laurence leave a strong impression on the reader. The presence in the story of Lucien, Mona and Marthe, for example, seems primarily designed to bring out certain features of Laurence's character or situation, and they are not themselves very well-developed or striking figures. They are rather one-dimensional because Laurence relates to each of them in only one major dimension. Her past and present feelings towards Lucien are explored in some detail, but virtually all that we learn about Lucien himself springs from his function as her lover in the story. We discover a little about his tastes and are given some impression of his professional competence, but the portrait of Lucien is wholly dominated by what is shown as an all-consuming passion for Laurence and his attempts to keep her. The book requires him to be a doomed romantic and a rather insubstantial figure ('Il vit dans un monde feutré, tout en nuances, en demi-teintes, en clair obscur'—**59**). Since Laurence herself admits to having used thoughts about him as 'une espèce d'alibi', and refers to the idea of missing him as 'une petite flamme romantique' (**146**), it is perhaps not surprising if the reader fails to engage with Lucien as an autonomous character in the story.

Another colleague of Laurence, Mona, is an equally shadowy character, albeit in a different way. We are told that, in contrast to Laurence, she is from a very modest background and has heavy family responsibilities (**68**), and we are given—without any details— the impression that she has a certain social or political commitment. We see very little of her in the novel, but her visit to Laurence's home (**67-71**) serves a clear purpose, in that it constitutes a rare moment in which Laurence is forced to look at her materially comfortable way of life from the outside. She is aware of a certain hostility in Mona, but tries to convince herself that Mona is 'sectaire' and that with 'un peu de bonne volonté' they would see eye to eye (**71**). The reader knows that this is not so, and is also heartened by Mona's resistance to Jean-Charles's general optimism (**73-74**). Later, when Laurence comes to accept Mona's view that the technocrats have no understanding of the suffering in the world (**133**; cf. **70**), it is doubly clear that Mona's role in the book is to be virtually the only representative of the strata of French society below the bourgeoisie. Yet none of this makes Mona into a well-defined character. If it would be an exaggeration to claim that she is no more than a mouthpiece, very little indeed is left once one takes away her strictly thematic function in the narrative.

The portrait of Laurence's younger sister, Marthe, is an equally one-dimensional one. Almost everything that we know about her relates to her conversion to religion. Laurence presents her from this angle from the first, contriving to hint that Marthe's Christian faith may be less than wholly authentic (9). In fact, Laurence seems to feel less charitable towards her sister than towards almost anyone else around her; the viciousness extends to her view of Marthe's husband, Hubert (9). It is true that the father's attitude to Marthe is identical with Laurence's (105), and it is clear that, thematically, Marthe serves to bring into the book ideas about the Christian upbringing of children that Laurence can be shown as firmly rejecting (75-77; 174). Nevertheless, we may still find something gratuitously offensive and artistically inadequate in the portrayal of Marthe, who is said to be only 'un instrument entre les mains de Dieu' (150), but looks, to the reader, more like a puppet in the hands of the author.

The three major characters in the novel—other than Laurence herself—who are given some depth are, of course, her father, mother and husband. Each functions as another representative of the French bourgeoisie, but each also has a vital and unique role in Laurence's life and development.

The fact that she is unable to find any particular reason why she should have married Jean-Charles rather than anyone else does not mean that he fails to stand out as an individual in the story. In his attitudes to the world, he typifies the French technocracy at least as much as any other character. Indeed, within the story, it is Jean-Charles above all who establishes what belonging to that category amounts to. Yet he does so convincingly, because we see him in a variety of situations—social, domestic and professional—and make out a cohesive and coherent figure, who is more than a mere point of reference in Laurence's thinking. Another important factor is that Jean-Charles does not just reactively share the prevailing confidence in the future: he is a positive enthusiast ('Inexplicablement, ça le ravit, ces merveilles à venir qu'il ne verra jamais de ses yeux'—11). But this is not to say that all of his views are held with such commitment, for sometimes we do have the impression that he is merely echoing current clichés. And there are certainly points at which his optimism is exposed as facile, as when he talks of men being '«enracinés planétairement»' (40); when he claims that prediction is becoming '«une science exacte»' (148); and especially whenever he is explaining things away to the children (30-31).

As this mixture of the genuine and the imitative may suggest, Jean-Charles is somewhat more complex than he may at first appear to be. At least earlier on in the story, Laurence regards him as a near-perfect husband (67). Yet from the first we see that the preoccupation with money that he shares with the other technocrats can cause him to be irritable at home and often overrides the concern that he ought to have for individuals. Laurence should have been less surprised to discover that he thinks she ought to have knocked the cyclist down to avoid expensive damage to the car (103; 134). Jean-Charles's evident lack of sympathy for Dominique's plight, moreover, is tempered only by his awareness that her abandonment by Gilbert has significant financial implications (119). It is suggested, too, that in forcing a present upon Laurence he is attempting to buy his way out of an argument between them (141), although, characteristically, Laurence later stops a little short of accepting this worst possible view of him (143).

By the end, however, it is not only Jean-Charles's obsession with money that is seen to make him less than 'le mari idéal'. For one thing, Laurence comes to have a major grievance against him concerning his attitude towards their children. He has obviously played relatively little part in their development (this is one of the reasons why his intervention when Catherine performs less well at school seems objectionable—130-3), and he clearly intimidates Catherine. It is, finally, when he fails to take seriously the matter of Catherine's friendship with Brigitte that Laurence feels obliged to make her stand (181-2). By then he has, in any case, lost a great deal of Laurence's respect. The ways in which she deceives him might already be said to be some kind of response to his failure to take much interest in her personally (60), but when, in an outburst, he indicates that the sympathy he had shown towards Laurence during a crisis was not, after all, based upon a shared concern over human suffering (133), we see him in a much harsher light. We may also remember Laurence's comment that in an earlier crisis he had agreed to her taking up a job because of the money it would bring in (19). We have little confidence that his wish to prevent another breakdown at almost any cost is wholly motivated by concern for his wife.

Jean-Charles by now seems a more fragile character than was apparent from the first. The inflexibility that leads him to hate the unexpected (55; 163), his need to win arguments (130), and his unwillingness to talk about his past (42) begin to add up to a personality not so very much more stable and secure than Laurence's: 'si autoritaire, si sûr d'avoir raison, et le moindre imprévu suffit à l'effrayer' (181). In obvious ways, he has dominated Laurence and, like Dominique, tried to make her conform to a particular image that he has of her (133). Yet there are signs that he needs her too, so that the moments when he expresses concern about her cannot be dismissed as wholly inauthentic, although whether any of this amounts to 'love' on his part is precisely the kind of question that Laurence's own reflections raise in the book. It is she, too, who sees that, for all his dynamism, success and optimism, he is not really a happy man (83). To the extent that he represents the French technocrats of the 1960s, he has to suffer from the kind of strains that Beauvoir saw them all as undergoing, but there are touches of complexity in his characterization that make him a good foil to Laurence in the novel.

The senses in which Laurence's mother Dominique also proves much more fragile than she first seems are obvious enough, but Beauvoir nevertheless makes her into a memorable and rather formidable character. Dominique is of course riding high at the beginning of the story. She has had to make her own way in life by sheer effort, by brushing others aside, and by catching one of the biggest fish in French society, Gilbert (9). But, at fifty-one, she is hostess to the rich, proud of her personal achievements, and still anxious to outdo everyone else socially. From the first, we see a definite hardness in her, as she criticizes her ex-husband (whom she abandoned as soon as her younger daughter married—9) for his lack of ambition, and refusal to help his nephew (15). Yet her pride seems to generate certain standards of behaviour—'«on ne se conduit pas comme une midinette»' (8)—and she appears as powerful a force to the reader as she does to those around her. It is made clear that she has wholly dominated Laurence's upbringing (20; 22; 33), to the extent that Laurence now has difficulties in relating to her. But we also learn that she was particularly good when Laurence was disturbed (25).

Yet this whole picture of success and dominance is shattered by Gilbert's decision to abandon her for a young girl. Far from deploring the loss of someone she 'loves', Dominique is wholly preoccupied with her loss of social status and financial security. When 'violence' gains the upper hand over 'douceur' in her (72), she becomes vicious and vulgar to the point where Laurence scarcely recognizes her. The vile letter that she writes to the young Patricia—on any account, an innocent participant in the events—is, apart from anything else, a bad misjudgement. But, above all, it shows that Dominique has lost control not simply over those around her (125), but also over herself. There is now some temptation to see her as a thoroughly disreputable, unpleasant, even somewhat satanic figure.

Laurence herself talks of her 'halo maléfique' (52), and claims: 'il
fait si noir dans ce cœur, des serpents s'y tordent' (117). The novel
as a whole, however, qualifies this view in a number of ways.
Perhaps the fact that Dominique is repaid in kind by Gilbert
(through humiliation—124) is the least important of these. More
significant is the fact that much emphasis is laid on Dominique's age.
From the first, she makes it clear that the years of struggling for
success and, latterly, the need to keep up social appearances in order
to hang on to Gilbert have taken their toll (16), so that at least we
understand her worry that Gilbert was her '«dernière chance»' (51).
Here, of course, Beauvoir is giving a general significance to
Dominique's plight and making a feminist point. Odious Dominique
may be, but she is in some measure the product of a society that
makes women work harder for success than men, and encourages
women to think in terms of catching and hanging on to their men for
their own security (114-5). And now, as she stresses to Laurence,
she risks being the victim of that same society, which dictates that
'«Socialement une femme n'est rien sans un homme»' (142; cf. 176).
It is the potential solitude of Dominique that comes strongly to the
fore after the final, unedifying break with Gilbert ('Une masse de
relations: pas une amie'—98); and the combination of solitude and
age is certainly made to elicit sympathy on her behalf: '«vieille et
seule: c'est atroce»' (115).

But even this is not the book's final word concerning Dominique.
Her very viciousness was itself the sign of a spirited rather than a
pale, feeble personality of the type we see elsewhere in this milieu—
'«J'aime mieux être odieuse que ridicule»' (118)—and it is extremely
difficult to feel wholly ill-disposed toward someone who, humiliated
as she has been, can take a certain maniacal pleasure at having ruined
Gilbert's wedding night: '«Je pense tout de même que je leur aurai
un peu gâché leur nuit de noces»' (127). This is, indeed, no more
than the first indication that Dominique will spring back, in spite of
all. It is true that she needs drugs to keep her going at the end
(although, as we have seen, in this she is not very different from
other technocrats), but the fact is that, in taking up life with her ex-
husband again, she appears to have found a new way of countering
the solitude that continues to obsess her. Socially, her prestige is
virtually restored and, perhaps above all, she has found herself a new
role to play (178). Whatever its quality, Dominique's very self-
renewal at the end is evidence of an energy, even perhaps of a love
of life, desperately lacking in Laurence. Albeit on a much reduced
scale, Beauvoir has created in Dominique a splendid figure with
many of the properties of a Balzac character.

The same cannot be said of Laurence's (unnamed) father. Clearly the reader needs, sooner or later, to form a separate assessment of him, by disregarding the fact that Laurence (and, to a lesser extent, Marthe) consider him to be so exceptional. And it is true that certain 'facts' about his past are available. His legal studies led him to a high-level clerical post in the French parliament (15); he has had illnesses, and was in a prisoner-of-war camp for four years (85); he had a difficult time with Dominique when the children were young and was eventually abandoned by her (9-10); and he has an abiding interest in music, literature and ancient cultures. We also see that, unlike Dominique, he maintains a strong interest in his grandchildren and is very good with them (37-38). Equally, looking at him coolly, we can see that he is capable of speaking very harshly about others (34; 105), and we may even find in him from the beginning a certain pomposity that prevents us from sharing Laurence's unreservedly high regard for him. But he fails to make a strong, independent impression upon us for most of the book and we remain primarily interested in him as a representative of 'passéiste' views. Then towards the end we are made to see him in a different light, as Laurence herself comes to change her mind about him.

In his regular arguments with Jean-Charles and others, Laurence's father clearly speaks not just in the name of the past as opposed to the future ('Jean-Charles vit déjà en 1985, papa regrette 1925'—41), but also, apparently, on behalf of certain basic humanist truths and values (149-50). To this extent, even if he does not have the command of facts possessed by his son (41), the reader is almost bound to sympathize with many of his ideas. His worries that the world is becoming '«inhumain»' (40) are unlikely to be dismissed by us as easily as by Jean-Charles, and he is certainly right to be sceptical about the kind of predictions for the future of man so beloved of the technocrats (148). His gloomy view of the present ('dans tous les pays l'homme est écrasé par la technique, aliéné à son travail, enchaîné, abêti'—84) is an extreme one, but no more absurd than Jean-Charles's naive optimism. Even as the father formulates his general solutions to the world's problems, however, the reader is less than convinced. His reference to poorer countries where people are allegedly content with 'un minimum vital', and his suggestion that the real answer is a moral revolution on the purely individual scale (84) leave even Laurence highly dubious (85).

Perhaps before Laurence herself, we already feel uneasy about this mysterious figure of a father who is supposed to hold the secret to everything, but whose very sanctimoniousness sets us on our guard: '«Je dois être un vieil idéaliste impénitent: j'ai toujours essayé de mettre ma vie en accord avec mes principes»' (35). But, in any case, the trip to Greece eventually reveals a different man altogether. As Laurence sees at the time, his great knowledge and genuine enthusiasm for Greek culture do not prevent him from being taken in by the standard tourist traps (156); and his superiority over the sightseers that he mocks is minimal (160). His claim that modern Greeks, like his other contemporaries, are uninteresting seriously undermines the view that he is a humanist; and, worse, he is positively hypocritical in his dealings with a Greek socialist ('on l'aurait cru inscrit au parti communiste'—165). Contradictions in his attitudes and 'values' are strongly to the fore by the end. He is about to give up his beloved solitude in order to live with Dominique again; in order to agree with her, he goes back on his previous opposition to psychiatry (159; 174-5); and, to Laurence's amazement, he consents to speak on the state radio system that he has previously castigated (35; 177).

Beauvoir was clear about the thematic reasons for portraying Laurence's father in just this way:

> Ce faux sage veut ignorer lui aussi le malheur des hommes: il utilise sa culture pour s'assurer un confort moral qu'il préfère à la vérité. Il est beaucoup moins insensible qu'il ne le prétend à la fortune, au succès, et ne recule pas devant les compromissions. Son remariage avec son ex-femme manifeste la collusion entre la bourgeoisie traditionnelle et la nouvelle: c'est une seule et même classe. (*TCF*, 174)

That this pattern emerges from the book can hardly be denied in a general way, but this does not amount to saying either that Laurence's father is a wholly convincing character, or that our attitude towards him is the same as our attitude towards the technocrats. For, as we have seen, he unquestionably speaks out on behalf of many values that most readers would wish to defend against those of the technocrats. Moreoever, a careful scrutiny of Beauvoir's statements about her character (and she felt obliged to correct the impression that he was expressing her own values) shows that she, too, saw more to commend in his views (which we must distinguish from his personality) than in those of Jean-Charles and company. How else can we interpret her comment (*TCF*, 172) that Laurence's scepticism about the values of the society she lives in comes from her father? It seems reasonable to suggest, then, that there is a certain ambiguity in Beauvoir's own attitude towards the father, or his functions in the novel, and that this results in a portrayal that is somewhat lacking in conviction. In any case, the fact is that, seeing the father through Laurence's own eyes, we have quite peculiar difficulty in disentangling a character from her vision of him. The difficulty is a special one, because the development of Laurence's attitude towards her father is of such central importance in the story. There is a major dimension to his presence in the story that can be explored only in relation to Laurence's personal psychology.

Laurence

The events narrated in *Les Belles Images* take place over a period of five months or so (from October 1965 to the following February or March), but there are many highly significant references back to happenings long before this period, so that a full understanding of the character of Laurence has to take these into account. The references are at no point systematically pulled together by Laurence herself or by anyone else in the book. It is the reader herself/himself who must perform the task of reconstructing Laurence's past. This specific requirement of the reader is a distinctive feature of the book and one that Beauvoir was well aware of. It is one major aspect of what she had in mind in talking of the reader's need to 'lire entre les lignes'.

Because most of the references back come to the reader through Laurence's own thoughts, it is clear that Laurence, too, sees the need to explain her present situation and state of mind in the light of the past. To some extent the process is presented as being bound up with psychoanalytical concepts and techniques. At the beginning of the final chapter, in lying down, drawing the curtains, and setting out to go back over every detail of the holiday with her father, Laurence is obviously engaging in what is, in a semi-technical sense, self-analysis. (One could even talk of 'abreaction', in connection with the final moment of the analysis at which she recognizes and discharges particular emotion aimed at her father, and then falls asleep exhausted by the effort—**179-80**). Her need to do so arises from the fact that she is undergoing a mental crisis that has issued in anorexia, as Jean-Charles confirms: '«On n'est pas anorexique sans raison: trouve la raison»' (**169**). Here, however, Laurence is analysing only the holiday with her father and its aftermath. In general, her reading of her present state of mind in relation to her past, is shown to be less than wholly reliable, so that the reader has not only to reconstruct her past, but also to interpret Laurence's own interpretation of it.

The following is a brief attempt to put together some of the more significant points that we learn about Laurence's past. It would be doubly misleading to think of them as 'facts', not only because we need to remember that Laurence is no more than a fictional character in a story, but also because we learn many of these things from her own thoughts. Even so, some points crosscheck with statements and comments by different characters in the book, and others that do not are given a certain plausibility by what we learn about particular characters and situations. In short, something like the following account has to be assumed in order to make coherent sense of a wide variety of references in the narrative.

Laurence was born around 1935. Her mother dominated her upbringing, both because she was determined that Laurence should always present the appropriate image and mix with the right people, and because Laurence's father was away from home for four years as a prisoner during the Second World War (**85**). Even in the years immediately after the war, Dominique insisted on taking Laurence off on holiday without her father, because she wanted to go to 'smart' places. Around 1945, when Dominique began working (for French radio), but above all when news of the extermination of the Jews and other horrors of the war were making their greatest impact in France, Laurence underwent a major emotional crisis ('tant d'horreur pour rien'—**25**), a crisis that she now sometimes calls to mind (in 1965) because her own daughter Catherine, at the same age, is beginning to cry at night, apparently for a similar reason.

At the age of nineteen, Laurence met Jean-Charles and she married him about a year later. Because Catherine is nearly eleven late in 1965, and also, perhaps, because Laurence claims that she did not exactly decide her own marriage (**119**), and refers to severe financial difficulties early on (**66**), the reader may suppose that the marriage was precipitated by Laurence's pregnancy. In any case, her early marriage and motherhood constituted a violent emotional shock that rather set back her mental development (**45**). We are not told how soon after Catherine her second daughter, Louise, was born, but we know that some three years after Laurence's marriage her mother left her father and began her liaison with Gilbert Mortier. Around 1960, Laurence experienced another depressive crisis (to which there are at least five substantive references in the text). Her mother and husband encouraged her to take on a job with an advertising agency, work that she enjoyed and which brought her some kind of stability for a time. Nevertheless, two years later a news story about a woman tortured to death once more disturbed her profoundly.

This is the background against which the events of the five
months of the narrative take place. The anorexia that Laurence
suffers in chapter IV (foreshadowed by earlier attacks of nausea) is
thus associated with the latest in a line of mental crises and has to be
understood and judged in relation to them. We are bound to see
Laurence's state of mind between the beginning of the book and the
anorexia as broadly the state she has been in since the crisis of 1962,
and even perhaps as typical of how she has been since starting work
after the earlier crisis in 1960. In any case, the story itself shows her
being brought under increasing pressure from a number of
directions. Catherine's anxieties are a serious worry to her, and
while Dominique is abandoned by her lover, Laurence chooses to
break with her own lover. Furthermore, both her husband and her
father disappoint her greatly during these five months.

It is as we watch Laurence struggling with her 'current' problems
that we come to see that such mental stability as she has attained as
fragile, and come to understand the nature of her vulnerability. It is
clear that the strain of conforming to the image of her projected by
her mother, then later by Jean-Charles and others, has been
considerable. The picture that we build up of Laurence is one of a
woman who gives most of the public signs of being in control of
herself and her life—she apparently has a happy married life, she is
professionally successful, and she is much sought after socially—but
is in fact always close to the point of losing that control. We learn
not just of her breakdowns in the past, but also of her bursts of
energy or explosions of passion (with Lucien as well as Jean-
Charles), which burn out rather quickly and leave her feeling flat,
perhaps cold, even depressed ('Elle s'est beaucoup dépensée, c'est
pour ça que maintenant elle se sent déprimée, je suis cyclique'—**8**).
And as the particular crises of the book crop up, we actually see her
struggling for control over her emotions, employing a variety of
techniques, some of which have presumably helped her through
more recent troubles, but others of which she has been encouraged to
adopt ever since her childhood. The text undermines in a number of
ways her own claim that the latter have been perfectly successful
(**132**), and when she ignores them the result is heartening for her:
'Boire un verre d'eau, faire de la gymnastique: non. Cette fois elle se
donne à sa colère; [...] c'est une douleur physique, mais on se sent
vivre'(**134**). Hence Lucien's charge that Laurence is unable to feel
emotions at all is badly misplaced. Indeed, her lucidity in
distinguishing between 'love' and sexual passion (as well as her
insistence that what looks like love from the outside may be nothing

of the sort) reveals a better understanding of emotion than he has. She is by no means an obvious victim of the myths about love that patriarchal society presses women to accept. Nevertheless, our recognition that something is amiss in relation to Laurence's ability to feel in general and to love in particular, and her own acknowledgement of this, constitute essential elements of the novel. Perhaps the most graphic example is provided by her relationship with her mother. Throughout the story, but particularly when Dominique is distraught over Gilbert, Laurence is deeply affected by her mother's state of mind, yet unable to have the feelings towards her that she believes she ought to be having (17; 52; 115-7; 124).

At various points in the text, moreover, she records her inability to react to music, works of art, history, etc. Her ultimate view of herself appears to be that she is incapable of engaging in any kind of activity with the whole of her being: 'Cette femme qui n'aime personne, insensible aux beautés du monde, incapable même de pleurer, cette femme que je vomis'(181). And yet, also by Laurence's own admission, there are two major exceptions to the indifference or detachment that characterizes her attitudes in so many areas: her deep love for her father and her intense attachment to her children. The emphasis on these two factors in the book, moreover, leaves no room for doubt that they are considerably more fundamental than other aspects of her life and behaviour. They clearly take us to the very heart of the character of Laurence.

From the broad structure of the novel and the later parallels with the psychoanalytical process, one might easily be led to suppose that it is Laurence's relationship with her father that constitutes the whole key to the story. After all, she was deprived of the kind of time with him that a child might be expected to need; and she thinks specifically in terms of a 'secret' to life possessed only by him. Moreover, there are a number of explicit references early on to the fact that, in her relations with men, she is seeking primarily to rediscover the love and tenderness that she felt and expressed as a young girl—perhaps all too briefly—for her father. The suggestion is that her relations with Jean-Charles and even Lucien have suffered for this very reason. Thus when, in connection with the trip to Greece related in chapter IV, there is mention of an unliquidated Oedipus complex, this is by no means unprepared for in the book, for Laurence has indicated that during an earlier crisis she had to acknowledge a deep-seated problem that brought her feelings for Jean-Charles into conflict with her feelings for her father (44). The Oedipal element might even be thought to be strengthened by the precise order of events in the last chapter, for her anorexia is brought on not by her eventual acknowledgement of the truth about the trip to Greece, but by the news that her father and mother, after some years of separation, are to live together again.

However, a very close reading of the book suggests that it would be a mistake to attach quite so much importance to a narrowly Freudian reading of the tale, and this is not surprising in the light of the ambivalent attitude of both Beauvoir and Sartre throughout their careers towards psychoanalytical theory. When Laurence finally admits to herself the true nature of the feelings that she experienced during the trip to Greece, she expresses them in terms to which it is difficult to give any sexual connotation:

> Je suis tout simplement jalouse. Œdipe mal liquidé, ma mère demeurant ma rivale. Électre, Agamemnon. Est-ce pour cela que Mycènes m'a tant émue? Non. Non. Billevesées. Mycènes était belle, c'est sa beauté qui m'a touchée. [...] Elle respire trop vite, elle halète. Ce n'était donc pas vrai qu'il possédait la sagesse et la joie et que son propre rayonnement lui suffisait! Ce secret qu'elle se reprochait de n'avoir pas su découvrir, peut-être qu'après tout il n'existait pas. Il n'existait pas: elle le sait depuis la Grèce. J'ai été *déçue*. Le mot la poignarde. [...] Je suis déçue. J'ai raison de l'être. **(179-80)**

As Laurence immediately goes on to say, the blow delivered by the news of the reconciliation taking place between her mother and father related, precisely, to her disappointment in him: Dominique's attention, and particularly the suggestion that he should speak on the radio, have flattered him and shown Laurence that he is as much given to contradiction and compromise as anyone else. To the reader, the alternative to believing that this is a broadly accurate account of Laurence's final state of mind is an implausible one. It would presumably involve supposing that Laurence is still fundamentally self-deceived about her father at the end of the novel, and perhaps that her stand over Catherine is therefore a fundamentally false one.

Our reluctance to adopt this alternative stems partly from a recognition of the centrality of Laurence's relations with her children, and of the obvious importance of the theme of upbringing in the book. The depth of Laurence's emotional involvement with her children again stands in outstandingly sharp contrast to her detachment and indifference in other areas. Her worries over Catherine are mentioned on the second page of the book; they figure very prominently in the rest of chapter I, and in chapter II; and they come to the fore once more late in chapter III, then in the last section of the final chapter.

A significant preliminary point to make is that these worries do centre very much on Catherine only. On a number of occasions Laurence shows appropriate concern for the well-being of Louise, but it is Catherine who dominates her thoughts about issues of upbringing, and this is not entirely because it is Catherine who has the problems. Firstly, Laurence openly admits that Catherine is her preferred daughter (**129**). And secondly, it is not wholly clear that Catherine's problems are as serious as Laurence takes them to be. We are surprised to learn that the crying during the night that so worries Laurence has happened only twice (**129**). When Jean-Charles insists that Catherine be sent to a psychiatrist, principally because she is doing less well at school than previously, Laurence objects. And the presumably objective view offered by the psychiatrist suggests that there is nothing particularly abnormal about Catherine, nothing dramatically wrong with her.

The fact is that Catherine, who is at exactly the age at which Laurence herself first became seriously disturbed by the horrors around her, becomes the principal focus of some of Laurence's own unresolved psychological difficulties. She admits that the whole matter is bound up in a complex way with the question of her feelings for her father, her marriage, and even her work (**43**); and we see early on that it is related to the controlling or avoidance of emotion discussed earlier. Since taking up a job she has relied upon Jean-Charles for her knowledge of current affairs, and her periodic attempts to catch up have been undermined by her profound fear of coming across some horror that will once more disturb her precarious balance (which is what appears to have happened in 1962):

> Elle replie le journal, soulagée tout de même, parce qu'on ne sait jamais ce qu'on risque d'y découvrir. J'ai eu beau me blinder, je ne suis pas aussi solide qu'eux. [...] j'ai horreur de me convulser, alors le mieux c'est d'éviter les occasions.(**44**)

Hence her first reaction to Catherine's distress is to stop her seeing what is disturbing her. Here we are at the very heart of all of Laurence's problems. There are some grounds for stressing their historical dimension, for it is hard to disagree with the view that there were good reasons for a child to lose her bearings in 1945, the time of Laurence's first major crisis (**25**).[3] Yet equally, more as she

---

[3] The character of Nadine in *Les Mandarins* illustrates the disturbing effects of being brought up during the war.

herself does, one may see Laurence's problem in universal, metaphysical terms:

> Pourquoi existe-t-on? Ce n'est pas mon problème. On existe. Il s'agit de ne pas s'en apercevoir, de prendre son élan, de filer d'un trait jusqu'à la mort. L'élan s'est brisé il y a cinq ans. J'ai rebondi. Mais c'est long le temps. On retombe. Mon problème, c'est cet effondrement de loin en loin, comme s'il y avait une réponse à la question de Catherine, une réponse effrayante. Mais non! C'est déjà glisser vers la névrose que de penser ça. Je ne retomberai pas. (**44**)

It may remain an open question whether, at their very deepest roots, Laurence's difficulties stem from an unresolved Oedipus complex, unavoidable metaphysical anguish, an upbringing in particularly difficult historical circumstances, or some combination of these. The fact remains that she has not yet solved them, as she periodically claims to have done. Her 'stability' at the end of chapter I ('il suffit d'un peu de vigilance pour que rien ne fissure cette sécurité'—**44**) comes under increasing threat, and her problems focus more and more on Catherine, as she abandons Lucien, as she loses all confidence in Jean-Charles, and as the reconciliation between her father and mother puts an end to her particular preoccupations with them as separate individuals.

Laurence's two major worries concerning Catherine are related in an obvious way, since her eventual insistence that Catherine be allowed to maintain her friendship with Brigitte is bound up with the decision to allow her daughter to be exposed to the outside world, rather than trying to protect her from it. But underlying both elements is Laurence's growing determination that Catherine should not be brought up in the way that she herself was brought up. She sees her own solitude as linked with the fact that she was prevented from choosing her own friends as a child (**174**); and in the end she decides not only that Catherine must have her friend, but more generally that her daughter's eyes, at least, must be opened to the world:

> Je ne permettrai pas qu'on lui fasse ce qu'on m'a fait. [...] au contraire lui ouvrir les yeux tout de suite et peut-être un rayon de lumière filtrera jusqu'à elle, peut-être elle s'en sortira... De quoi? De cette nuit. De l'ignorance, de l'indifférence. Catherine... Elle se redresse soudain.
> —On ne lui fera pas ce qu'on m'a fait. (**180-1**)

That there is something admirable about Laurence's final stance in the book is not open to serious doubt. At the very least she is eventually determined not to commit what can probably be regarded as the most common fault in parenthood: bringing up the child as a carbon copy of oneself. She also acknowledges her mother's errors and is set to avoid them, almost at all costs. But one of a number of worrying features of Laurence's stand is that it is, nevertheless, shown to constitute a repetition of certain broader patterns concerning her own upbringing, though not of the actual nature of it. For, in consciously reacting against the manner of her upbringing, she is engaging in a process very similar to the one that her own mother was involved in:

> Elle a toujours été une image. Dominique y a veillé, fascinée dans son enfance par des images si différentes de sa vie, tout entière butée—de toute son intelligence et son énorme énergie—à combler ce fossé. (Tu ne sais pas ce que c'est que d'avoir des souliers déchirés et de sentir à travers sa chaussette qu'on a marché sur un crachat. Tu ne sais pas ce que c'est d'être toisée par des copines aux cheveux bien lavés et qui se poussent du coude. Non, tu ne sortiras pas avec cette tache sur ta jupe, va te changer.) (21-22)

It is true that Laurence has now gone beyond an earlier stage, at which her concern for the state of Brigitte's skirt directly echoed her mother's obsessions, but the fact that the text shows her final stand over Catherine to be a reaction against a reaction against something else hints at the cyclical nature of patterns of upbringing, rather than suggesting that Laurence has arrived at a fully reasoned policy.

Moreover, Laurence's final attitude towards Jean-Charles's role in bringing up the children reinforces our impression that she is responding rather impulsively to her latest discoveries about the adults around her. After all, the logic of her comments on Jean-Charles's role ('«C'est moi qui m'occupe de Catherine. Toi tu interviens de loin en loin. Mais c'est moi qui l'élève, et c'est à moi de prendre des décisions. Je les prends»'—181-2) is questionable in the extreme. The psychiatrist has suggested that more involvement and effort is required on Jean-Charles's part; and, in principle, it is an odd and rather drastic reaction to a personal perception of a child's needs to seek to exclude the father from its upbringing.

On these issues, the ending of *Les Belles Images* is open to a number of different readings. We perhaps need to remember Beauvoir's deep scepticism about marriage and the family. On the least radical interpretation of her views, she believed that upbringing by the natural mother and father does not necessarily guarantee the wellbeing of the child, and that family circumstances not infrequently hinder or harm the child's development. Certainly, the problems of upbringing are not ones to which the book offers any semblance of a helpful solution. It may well be, in fact, that

Laurence expresses earlier the view that finally predominates in the book, when she muses on the difficulties of bringing up a child without religion in a society that presses religion upon it (76) and shows dismay at the knowledge that everything that parents do affects and marks the child in some way, without the process ever being fully under control (135-6).

In any case, the whole question of upbringing has to be replaced in the context of the novel as a whole. It is important to recognize that, in taking a stand over Catherine, Laurence is not simply reacting against Jean-Charles and her own upbringing. To some extent she is revolting against the values of the class to which her husband and her parents belong ('ils lui feront tout avaler; tout quoi? tout ce qu'elle vomit, sa vie, celle des autres avec leurs fausses amours, leurs histoires d'argent, leurs mensonges'—180). Even here, however, the nature of her revolt is tenuous and a little obscure, if only because her final stand, whatever its implications for the upbringing of Catherine, leaves Laurence's own unsatisfactory position unaltered. Her assertion that it is too late to rectify her own life ('«Moi, c'est foutu, j'ai été eue, j'y suis, j'y reste»'—181) echoes many of Beauvoir's post-1970 comments on the situation of many women, but it comes strangely from the mouth of a woman of thirty-one. If Laurence's revolt really is directed partly against the whole milieu in which she exists, there is already an oddity in the fact that it never seems to occur to her that she might change the nature of her work, which, after all, is shown to be closely bound up with some of the most objectionable features of modern capitalist societies. Equally odd is her continuing assumption (voiced earlier in the story) that she is permanently stuck with Jean-Charles, no matter what happens. And, more generally, there is no definite indication that Laurence, who has been shown as willing to lie in one way or another to all of those close to her, is now determined to deal with others more honestly and openly. In short, it is clear on a number of counts that Beauvoir is certainly not offering Laurence as a kind of model for her women readers. At best, the central figure of *Les Belles Images* makes, at the end of the story, one basic step towards greater lucidity about some aspects of her life. But, as with a number of Beauvoir's other protagonists, one is left unsure about how much progress has been made and with little substantive reason for great confidence in her future.

None of this is surprising if we see the relationship between Laurence and the class to which she belongs in the way in which Beauvoir herself claims to have set out to present it. She wanted to portray Laurence as partly absorbed into the stratum of society under scrutiny and partly alienated from, and resistant to it: 'une jeune femme assez complice de son entourage pour ne pas le juger, assez honnête pour vivre cette connivence dans le malaise' (*TCF*, 172). It is implied, as we have seen, that in Laurence's own upbringing, while Dominique encouraged Laurence to adopt bourgeois values, her father's influence worked against them. But, however that may be, part of the success of the novel consists in the very fact of placing Laurence in a deeply ambiguous position in relation to society. For this probably reflects the ambivalence felt by many readers towards the society in which they live and are in certain ways trapped. Already in *Les Mandarins*, Beauvoir was illustrating the impossibility of being morally in the right within a society that is fundamentally flawed in its economic and social structures, but at that stage, in the aftermath of war, the point had a very particular historical force. What is essentially the same perception in *Les Belles Images* is given an especially modern resonance.

Narrative technique and style

In connection with the composition of *L'Invitée*, Beauvoir wrote in her memoirs of a fundamental narrative principle adopted by Sartre and herself in the mid-1930s: 'à chaque chapitre, je coïncidais avec un de mes héros, je m'interdisais d'en savoir ou d'en penser plus long que lui' (*La Force de l'âge*, p. 386). That is, they believed that there is no place for a privileged observer in the novel; that at any given stage in a work of fiction the author should adopt the point of view of one of the characters in the story, strictly restricting herself/himself to what that character could have known and might have thought at that time. Yet it can easily be demonstrated that in some of their fiction this rule is frequently breached. Recent literary theory, in any case, suggests that the matter is more complicated, and that, even when an author is adopting the point of view of a character (using the character as a 'focalizer'), the presence of a narrator over and above the focalizer will still be discernible in the text. Nevertheless, both Sartre and Beauvoir hung on to their original principle, as they understood it, throughout their careers as writers of fiction, so that, in general, their narratives are characterized by the absence of free-standing descriptions, summaries and authorial psychological analysis, and by the use of dialogue as action. In any case, one has always to start by taking account of which character's viewpoint Beauvoir is adopting.

In *Les Belles Images,* as in each of the three stories of *La Femme rompue,* she confines herself to the perspective of only one (woman) character. This in itself is of some significance, for in all of her earlier novels (we can leave aside the stories of *Quand prime le spirituel,* which were probably written before any narrative principle was clearly formulated) she had attempted to see through the eyes of at least two characters; and twice she had alternated between one perspective and another in a regular and systematic fashion. It has recently been suggested that this particular technique was especially appropriate during the middle stage of Beauvoir's intellectual development,[4] but, however that may be, she was quite conscious of a significant change of approach when it came to writing *Les Belles Images:*

> Dans mes précédents romans, le point de vue de chaque personnage était nettement explicité et le sens de l'ouvrage se dégageait de leur confrontation. Dans celui-ci, il s'agissait de faire parler le silence. Le problème était neuf pour moi. (*TCF,* 172)

One must guard against the temptation of oversimplifying her earlier fiction, but it is clear that Beauvoir is right to claim that she is employing focalization in a markedly different way in this novel, and that this relates to her wish to discourage the reader from identifying too closely with the only character whose viewpoint is adopted.

We have already seen that the requirement upon the reader to reconstruct Laurence's past and to make her/his own judgement upon the character's version of her problems and their causes is built into the text. In other words, the narrative itself, though written from Laurence's point of view, contrives to show that point of view to be less than wholly reliable. This is an interesting, though not an especially unusual literary device, and it is hard to believe that Beauvoir's use of it had nothing at all to do with its prominence in the *nouveau roman* movement of the 1950s and early 1960s (in spite of her harsh comments on this movement). She subverts the authority of Laurence's viewpoint by making some of the character's assumptions and assertions contradict others, or conflict with actions and events. Thus, to take an obvious but central example, Laurence's belief that her psychological troubles are over ('Je suis au net avec moi-même'—**44**) is not only clearly shown by what happens

---

[4] Fallaize (1988), pp. 175-84.

subsequently to be mistaken, but is also perceived as being incompatible with what we have already learned, so that we are sceptical about the belief even when it is formulated. In addition to this, Laurence has from the first, as we have seen, a deeply and disturbingly ambivalent attitude towards the milieu to which she belongs, with the result that there is an intrinsically unsettled and unsettling quality to her perception of the world. Once we recognize, therefore, that the novel is strongly marked by Laurence's own conscious questioning and doubting of almost all that she does and says, we can see that the authority of her viewpoint is subverted at two levels: firstly by Beauvoir, who juxtaposes comments and events in such a way as to undermine some of Laurence's judgements; and secondly by the character herself, who displays an unstable vision and an almost permanent lack of faith in her own judgements.

Stylistically, the mixture of 'complicité' and 'malaise' in Laurence's attitude towards her bourgeois milieu produces a rather extraordinary range of devices, to which it is impossible to do justice here. The most prominent and probably the most complex is the use of both pronouns 'je' and 'elle' (together with the name Laurence) in what are ostensibly Laurence's references to herself. In some measure the distinction is that between seeing herself from the inside and from the outside, from her own standpoint or from society's. And since this is bound up with the extent to which Laurence does or does not conform to others' image of her, Beauvoir achieves some sharp effects by swapping from 'je' to 'elle', and vice versa, at crucial moments:

> Elle a toujours été une image. [...] Et Laurence et Jean-Charles de clair vêtus, hâlés, polis. Soudain, un soir, au retour d'une promenade, dans la voiture arrêtée, sa bouche sur ma bouche, cet embrasement, ce vertige. Alors, pendant des jours et des semaines, je n'ai plus été une image, mais chair et sang, désir, plaisir. [...] De nouveau, il y a dix-huit mois, avec Lucien; le feu dans mes veines, et dans mes os cette exquise déliquescence. Elle se mord la lèvre. Si Jean-Charles savait! En réalité rien n'a été changé entre Laurence et lui. (**21-22**)

Here both pronouns are used to refer to Laurence in the past, but there are also successful sequences in the text where 'elle' denotes the Laurence in the past being observed and commented upon by the 'je' of the narrative present. It is not surprising either, in the light of our earlier discussion of the repression of emotion, that there should be moments when the effect of the use of 'je' is to indicate emotion welling up in the apparently controlled Laurence/'elle', thereby highlighting her mental struggles. On the other hand, even her most violent 'present' emotions are sometimes described in the third person: 'Malgré elle, la voix de Laurence se monte [...]. Son cœur bat très fort, ses yeux brûlent' (**182**).

It has recently been shown that the avoidance of personal pronouns altogether at certain points in the text is a further factor to be taken into account.[5] The whole matter, moreover, is inextricably bound up with the almost equally complicated mixing of tenses in the text. But for the moment, in the absence of a very detailed study, it remains to be demonstrated that either device is used in a fully coherent and consistent way. Different purposes seem to be served by variations of pronoun and tense at different stages of the novel. No single way of explaining everything in terms of Laurence's state(s) of mind can be sustained throughout. A major aspect of the use of these stylistic devices, as with others, is how clearly they mark off chapter IV from the preceding chapters. 'Je' is the pronoun employed for virtually the whole of the long account of Laurence's self-analysis, which is consistently described in the past tense, because it centres on the trip to Greece from which she has returned. With her retrospective look at the trip completed, the brief but crucial final part of the novel reverts to the present tense, and once more there is oscillation between 'je' and 'elle'. In general, the text of the final chapter is, in its form, very much closer to a conventional first-person narrative than the rest of the book, but the nature of any 'resolution' of Laurence's problems contained in the last few pages is not such as to pull everything together and also resolve the stylistic questions just discussed.

Other outstanding stylistic features of the book present no special puzzles. The reasons why they should be largely absent from chapter IV and have the particular incidence that they do in the first three chapters, moreover, are not hard to see, since they relate, once more, to Laurence's distinctive kind of alienation from the values of those around her.

Particularly in those sequences where Laurence is in company, Beauvoir employs—sometimes generating a humour that is rare in her fiction—an impressive array of devices to display the patterns of thought of a character who is never more than partially immersed in the social game. Thus on the very first page of the text we find Laurence wondering, 'Qu'est-ce que les autres ont que je n'ai pas?' (**7**), and this thought is made to resonate throughout the novel, but with subtly significant variations. She relates it, for instance, to her perception of the special qualities of her father (**14**). Then later, she

---

[5] Fallaize (1988), pp. 122-3.

begins to think again: 'Il me manque quelque chose que les autres
ont... À moins... À moins qu'ils ne l'aient pas non plus' (**83**). Finally,
just before the serious tone of the final chapter banishes most general
thoughts of this kind, Laurence turns the observation on its head:
'qu'est-ce que j'ai qu'ils n'ont pas?' (**150**).

Also at the very beginning of the novel, we find, combined with a
self-questioning typical of Laurence, the first occurrence of a
powerful intuition that she will have from time to time throughout
the first three chapters:

> (Juste en ce moment, dans un autre jardin, tout à fait différent, exactement
> pareil, quelqu'un dit ces mots et le même sourire se pose sur un autre
> visage: «Quel merveilleux dimanche!» Pourquoi est-ce que je pense ça?) (**7-8**)

Where it occurs in connection with Dominique, it can be triggered
by a particular phrase or even a cry (**50**). And when Laurence is
with Lucien it can take the form of the suggestion that they are
simply going through the same motions as scores of other lovers:
'Juste à cette minute, des tas d'amants sont en train de rompre'
(**110**). The insight may be elevated on to an almost metaphysical
plane (**60**), but primarily it serves to cut characters and their
activities down to size, by implying that there is nothing unique
about them. It is similar to a recurring question asked by Laurence,
'«Pourquoi Jean-Charles plutôt que Lucien?» [...] (Pourquoi moi
plutôt qu'une autre?)' (**65**); and Beauvoir even has Laurence embed
the one thought within the other: '(Une autre jeune femme, des
centaines de jeunes femmes en cette minute se demandent: pourquoi
lui plutôt qu'un autre?)' (**137**). Both devices, too, are linked with
Mona's remark, which so surprises Laurence, that Jean-Charles and
Lucien are as alike as two peas in a pod—an observation that she
tellingly adopts and applies to her father and mother, when they are
reconciled: 'Il n'était pas d'une autre espèce. Mona me dirait: «Ben
quoi! c'est deux gouttes d'eau»' (**180**).

If all of these constitute devices that could be said to hinge
directly on Laurence's trains of thought as such, we can just as easily
locate a range of special techniques relating to the expression of
those thoughts. It is already clear from the particular examples
given, as well as from Beauvoir's intention not to describe the
experience of technocratic society, but to 'faire entendre ce qu'on
appelle aujourd'hui son «discours»' (*TCF*, 172), that the business of
(consciously or unconsciously) echoing and imitating, of quoting or
parodying others' very terms, is a prominent feature of *Les Belles*

Images. At the most general level, one could mention the vital importance of dialogue in the novel: a number of sparkling sequences simply bowl along under the momentum of the dialogue, without any interruption for the recording of Laurence's thoughts, and with the bourgeois characters condemning themselves from their own lips. But if Beauvoir, as it were from the outside, is imitating this élite, she also has Laurence imitating it from within, or from nearly within. Sometimes Laurence does so with detachment and deliberate irony, and she has a running joke with her father, at Dominique's expense: '—«Qui imite-t-elle en ce moment?»' (**34**). But this is a joke that risks rebounding on Laurence in the text, not just because its reiteration itself becomes an imitation, but also because, although she sometimes just stops herself before using the egregious terms of those around her (**69**), on other occasions she falls into that trap without being aware of it.

More striking and typical of the novel, however, are the numerous devices of expression whereby Laurence's own thoughts and feelings are shown to turn back upon, and undermine themselves.[6] Sometimes it is a matter of her private thoughts undermining her public words. This may be because she wishes to convey an inauthentic impression, either in company ('«J'aime bien écouter de la musique.» (Ce n'est pas vrai, en fait. Je dis ça pour être drôle)'—**12**), or to a particular person, as when, amusingly, she tries to preserve her mother's feelings: 'Évidemment elle n'a plus quarante ans. «Tu n'as plus vingt ans, évidemment,» dit Laurence' (**16**). But there is frequently a sense in which one of Laurence's thoughts or feelings is qualifying, correcting, questioning or contesting another. Questions as such play a part in this process and therefore proliferate in the text. If many of the issues concerned are relatively trivial, the specific kind of self-questioning involved can also be used to show significant puzzlement ('Si je la connaissais, ça m'aiderait peut-être (à quoi?)'—**71**), as well to develop serious themes, such as Laurence's concern about Catherine: '«Oui je lui ai ressemblé,» dit Laurence. (Me ressemblera-t-elle?)' (**105**).

Yet questions in the literal sense constitute just one of a number of ways in which the text has Laurence directly challenging her own words or thoughts. She often corrects herself, either over the appropriateness of a particular word (**10**), or over her very reactions: 'Ils rient, ils plaisantent, et elle ne trouve pas leurs plaisanteries drôles. L'an dernier... Eh bien! elle ne s'était pas

---

[6] There is fairly detailed discussion of these and other stylistic devices in the introduction to Stefanson's edition of *Les Belles Images*.

beaucoup amusée non plus, mais elle avait fait semblant' (**145-6**). And even on the most important matters she queries or qualifies her own perceptions as readily as she does those of others: 'Le silence ressemble à une complicité; il exprime un accord trop profond pour les mots. Illusion peut-être' (**20**). Asides of all kinds are a marked feature of the narrative, which consequently depends heavily upon brackets in the text and occasionally uses suspension marks to good effect (**9**). The omission of quotation marks where they would seem to be appropriate also keeps the reader working, since there can sometimes be fruitful ambiguity about the source of particular remarks.

Where a number of these devices are strung together, the result can be disorienting for the reader. This is particularly the case in the very first paragraph of the novel, where the confusion is deliberately compounded by the fact that a framework of reference for the proper names and pronouns is not yet established. As we have seen, the participation of the reader is consciously sought by Beauvoir and it would not be difficult to show how the narrative proceeds by means of a succession of minor enigmas to be resolved: How has Catherine come to see the poster? When will Dominique learn everything about Gilbert's fiancée? What did Gilbert do when he assaulted Dominique? And so on. But there are major mysteries too, like the central one that Laurence is trying to unravel in chapter IV ('Qu'ai-je manqué? Je ne le sais même pas'—**153**) and, in general, it is clear that much of the book revolves around puzzling questions concerning the difference between appearance and reality, conduct and feelings, image and substance.

For 'image', as the title suggests, is of course a key word and concept in the novel. Examining its ramifications would take a study in its own right, but even by making the obvious distinction between image in the literal and metaphorical senses we can gain some idea of the importance of this feature of the book. The physical images dwelt upon in the text include: the magazine photograph of Feuverolles, Dominique's reflection in the mirror, publicity images, the view from the window in the hotel where the young Laurence was with Jean-Charles, Mona's sketches, the poster that distresses Catherine, the patterns created by a kaleidoscope, photos in an astronomy book, and television pictures. And, needless to say, crucial references to images in the metaphorical sense—mostly, but not exclusively, 'images' of people in the minds of other—are to be found at all stages of the narrative. We have seen that the way in which Dominique forced Laurence to conform to a certain image is central to the story, as is the latter's determination not to do the same with

Catherine: 'Élever un enfant, ce n'est pas en faire une belle image' (**182**). When things go wrong for Laurence, she thinks in terms of shattered images (**124**); and when she engages in self-analysis she expects that clarification will come partly through images: 'je récapitulerai ce voyage image par image, mot par mot' (**153**). Then there is the whole matter of Laurence's work, since the constant search for publicity images has resulted in a *déformation professionnelle*: 'Tout ce qu'elle touche se change en image' (**21**). (Beauvoir's choice of a profession for Laurence was an inspiration, for the character's ambivalence about technocratic society is crystallized in the way in which she must see through publicity images in order to exploit them commercially).[7] Thus, for instance, she can scarcely see the necklace that Jean-Charles insists on buying her, but only what it stands for. Similarly, the descriptions of expensive objects near the end of chapter III (**137-8**; **145**) are coloured by many aspects of the treatment of images in the book and here convey, above all, the obscene wealth of the bourgeoisie.

In short, there a great richness to this feature of the book, but it is a richness that is never out of control at the literary or stylistic level. In connection with 'images', Beauvoir handles repetitions, echoes, analogies and variations with considerable skill, leaving the interpretation of the concept open-ended, yet never stretching it so far that it becomes meaningless. Indeed, this kind of comment applies to all of the stylistic devices discussed. Beauvoir was aware of having given an unusual degree of literary care to the composition of *Les Belles Images*, and the result produced was well worth the pains taken. The techniques adopted and the detailed devices employed are blended together in a coherent and telling way. The style of the novel would undoubtedly repay closer study, for the devices touched upon here, together with the broad difference of style between chapters I-III and chapter IV, can all be seen to be subordinated to thematic considerations in a synthesis that makes the book one of Beauvoir's very highest literary achievements.

---

[7] For a discussion of this aspect of the book, see I. Pagès (1988).

Chapter Two

La Femme rompue

'L'Âge de discrétion'

In the early part of 'L'Âge de discrétion', the first of the three stories in *La Femme rompue*, Beauvoir is clearly taking up again the theme of upbringing, which was so central to *Les Belles Images*. The main character (she is unnamed, and we shall refer to her as Madame), through whose eyes we follow events, is a retired teacher with one child, a thirty-year-old son, Philippe. In the whole of Beauvoir's fiction, this is the only portrayal from the mother's point of view of the relationship between mother and grown-up son. In *Le Deuxième Sexe,* she had argued that a mother will often live vicariously through her son and that her influence on him will often be harmful, although he can fairly easily escape from her grasp.[1] These points are directly illustrated in 'L'Âge de discrétion', which begins with Madame eagerly awaiting her son's return from his honeymoon; shows the break between them over his decision to abandon his university career; and brings to light the ways in which the mother has tried to force him into her own academic mould.

The exact manner in which the rift comes about between them, though convincingly dramatized, is of little significance in itself, but Madame's subsequent reflections on her son's upbringing and her discussions on the subject with her husband, André, relate the plot in an interesting way to Beauvoir's preoccupation with the influence of childhood. We see, even while she is waiting for Philippe to return, that Madame is reluctant to let go of her married son (**11**), and that she has probably had to press him hard to continue his studies (**16**). She acknowledges with some puzzlement both that she was intensely anxious that he should become an intellectual and that she held out against her husband on the issue (**20**). There prove to be strong echoes of the particular kind of tyranny that Dominique exercised over Laurence in some of Madame's memories of Philippe's childhood (**23**), but her 'victory' over him proves even less secure than Dominique's, for the understanding that she claims to have

---

[1] *Le Deuxième Sexe,* II, pp. 331-2.

eventually reached with Philippe is fragile enough to be shattered by his decision to change careers.

In subsequently looking back on how she brought up her son, Madame recognizes that there has always been a 'sourde opposition' between herself and André over Philippe (**29**), but claims that it is she who has shaped Philippe's life (**27**). She also has her own account of André's allegedly unhelpful participation in the upbringing, talking of the 'classique rivalité père-fils' and arguing that André has always underestimated Philippe and pushed him towards mediocrity (**29**). Yet once Madame has come to see the inevitability of her son's independence, and has even begun to voice reservations about Philippe that she claims to have had for some time (**32**; **34**), much of the interest of this aspect of 'L'Âge de discrétion' centres on the extent to which discussions with André may produce a different view of Philippe's upbringing and evolution. André, in fact, makes a number of points of which Madame seems previously to have taken little account. He reminds her that there were earlier signs of Philippe's change of values (**36**), and points out that both Madame's ambition and his own attitude to Philippe made things difficult for the boy. His suggestion that they each bear some responsibility for how Philippe has turned out appears to be accepted by Madame, who eventually talks of the role of both parents ('«Un enfant [...] devient ce que le font ses parents»'—**44**). She also takes the analysis a little further, in a way that again echoes *Les Belles Images,* when she suggests that her own upbringing has been a factor in her attitudes: '«Dans ma jeunesse on m'a tellement donné tort, avoir raison m'a tant coûté, que je répugne à me critiquer»'(**44**). (She had already acknowledged that it was because books had been her own salvation during her childhood that she rated culture so highly—**20**.)

In short, a number of elements in the story come together to indicate that upbringing is a more complex process than Madame apparently assumed. It is noticeable, for instance, that a little outburst from Philippe himself is recorded, in which he claims that he actually sacrificed some of his own ambitions in order to satisfy his mother (**56**). This is perhaps a timely reminder that, if both parents bear responsibility for a child's upbringing, for better or worse the child, too, plays an active part in it. And, of course, the older the 'child' becomes, the more we must acknowledge that s/he is an autonomous human being making free choices: long before the end of the story it is abundantly clear that Philippe is not going against the grain in choosing a new career, and that his views have definitely changed over a period of time (**55**). We also have an 'external' view on this particular case of upbringing, for André's mother claims that it is because the parents no longer believe in anything very much that Philippe has come to adopt his rather pusillanimous position(72). This is rather hard on André and Madame, whose very energy and success in life may have been an important factor. But what the criticism brings out is yet another element in Philippe's evolution, namely historical and political circumstances, as André confirms: '«tu parles de l'Algérie: il a été drôlement déçu. Pas un des types pour qui il s'est mouillé ne lui a donné signe de vie. Et le grand homme là-bas, c'est de Gaulle»'(79). The theme of upbringing, then, which seemed of central importance at the beginning of the story, is gradually set into a much wider context as the plot progresses.

Beauvoir herself claimed (*TCF,* 176) that the core of the story is the rift between Madame and André, and that the issue of Philippe's decision should be seen as what occasions it. The broad structure of the story bears this out. The narrative is divided into five sections by gaps in the text. The first two—the shortest—centre mainly on Madame's attitude towards her son, but by early in the third section the break between them is effected (**35**). This is not the end of the matter, of course, nor even Madame's last contact with Philippe, but it already marks a shift of emphasis to relations between the parents, for disagreements immediately arise concerning both how to understand what has happened and how to react to it. The rest of the third section is dominated by the quarrel between Madame and André, although by the end of the section—exactly halfway through the text (**47**)—there is a temporary reconciliation between them, which clearly prefigures the end of the story proper. In the fourth section, however, relations between them worsen again, for reasons that have little to do with Philippe. During a separation of a fortnight or so, Madame turns in on herself and comes to question every aspect of her life. It is only in the final section, when she rejoins André, that good relations between them are restored. At the end, their long-standing relationship is seen as their very best hope for the future: 'Nous sommes ensemble, c'est notre chance' (**84**).

Again, many of the details concerning their quarrel and eventual reconciliation, while perfectly plausible in context and by no means lacking in human interest, can be left aside here. Beauvoir, deliberately taking up ideas current in the mid-1960s, makes some play with the notions of communication and non-communication (**9**), for Madame's opening confidence in her ability to communicate is soon shown to be misguided. The story somewhat mechanically shows that it is her misinterpretation of certain of André's words and actions that prolongs the disagreement between them. In this sense, their quarrel comes to seem like a storm in a teacup. But two broad features of what happens between them raise their squabble to one of some general interest: the nature of Madame's struggle to see things clearly, and the theme of ageing.

The phenomenon of 'mauvaise foi', or self-deception, is of the greatest importance in both Beauvoir's fictional and non-fictional works, and reference to it is indispensable to an understanding of the mentality of Madame. Over many of the points already touched upon in connection with her relations with Philippe and André, it is made clear that she has been deceiving herself. As far as Philippe is concerned, we saw that she does not wish to believe that he no longer belongs to her (**11**); and her eventual recognition that she had to push him into an academic career implies that for many years she tried to persuade herself that this was what he wanted. Similarly, virtually everything that she thinks about Philippe's wife, Irène, provides evidence of Madame's persistent attempts to delude herself. She tries to blind herself to her daughter-in-law's very existence and put the clock back (**22**); and she attempts to convince herself that Philippe will never love such a woman (**23**); or that, in spite of the fact that she is typical of the 'femmes élégantes, distantes, snobs' whom he has always sought out, Irène has particular features that make her the source of all of the current problems (**29**). André not only sees through this last mental manoeuvre, but on two occasions convincingly charges Madame with pretending to herself that her hurt feelings are moral criticisms of Philippe (**35**; **75**). He also spots and describes the general basis of Madame's 'mauvaise foi': '«Par optimisme, par volontarisme, tu te caches la vérité et quand elle te crève enfin les yeux, tu t'effondres ou tu exploses»'(**43**). But, as readers, we see that it can also take other forms. Thus she talks, for instance, of her belief in culture, which she 'n'arrive pas à considérer [...] d'un œil critique'(**20**); and of all the suspicions about Philippe that she had 'refoulés' (**34**).

Yet one of the reasons for not over-emphasizing the importance of 'mauvaise foi' in this particular story is that Madame commonly recognizes it in herself and, to this extent, counters it. Many of the above examples can be seen to have been unmistakable instances of self-deception only because she herself sees through them. This is not just retrospective, in the sense that she comes to realize that she has deceived herself about Philippe in the past and thereby breaks the spell, for we can sometimes watch her simultaneously beginning to adopt a self-deluding strategy and recognizing it as such, as when she becomes aware that something is troubling André: 'Quelque chose le rongeait, que moi j'ignorais. Que je ne souhaitais pas connaître, qui m'effrayait' (50). In the time-span of the story Madame's lucidity is virtually a match for her 'mauvaise foi'. She reaches the more unpleasant truths about herself almost as soon as we do, and this is why her own implicit references to her stubbornness, her rigidity, her arrogance, her pride, her pig-headed optimism, and her irascibility, as well as her acceptance of these charges when they are made by others, are as much the key to understanding her problems as is the process of self-deception.

Furthermore, we need to remember that self-deception is one thing and making a genuine mistake quite another. An instructive case here is the development of Madame's attitude towards the latest book she has written. She is particularly pleased with it when the story begins, believing that she has broken new ground and forged a new method of literary criticism (18-19). However, as a result of unfavourable comments, as well as her own rereading of it, she becomes convinced that it is a complete failure: 'Inutile. À jeter au feu' (63). Yet it would be hasty to assume that Madame has been deceiving herself about her latest work. Is it not simply that she has formed a mistaken assessment of its value? What tells us more about her character than the supposition that she is self-deluded about her writing is the fact that she leaps from one extreme to the other; from believing it is her best work to believing that it is entirely worthless. André, as so often, offers a more balanced view: that, though interesting, it is less different from her earlier works than she thought; that she works better on a specific project than when her main objective is to do something new.

This whole matter is significant because it is closely bound up with Madame's worry that she and André may have reached a stage in their lives when they can no longer be genuinely creative. This, in turn, is just one aspect of the theme of ageing, which Beauvoir describes (TCF, 176) as lying at the origin of the story. She also admits that she scarcely skimmed the surface of a subject that was far too vast for so short a text, and to the extent that she was to go on to produce, in 1970, a detailed two-volume study of old age, La Vieillesse, we can understand her comment. But the story cannot be expected to make a significant contribution to the sociological understanding of old age, and it rarely strays into that territory. The details and statistics inserted near the beginning (12) stand out extremely awkwardly. On the other hand, the point made near the end that Madame and André hold an extremely privileged and cushioned position within the category of older people is brought in quite naturally when André comes back into contact with his poorer contemporaries (**73**). It is true, nevertheless, that there is something irritating in Beauvoir's particular manner of raising, but leaving hanging in the air, some aspects of the topic of old age. (Is it true that only young scientists produce original work? Do people of sixty or so have to regard sex as an activity from which they are excluded?) Yet none of this amounts to saying that a story of these dimensions can cast no light on the subject. If we stress the theme of ageing rather than that of old age, it can still be said that 'L'Âge de discrétion' constitutes a quite penetrating illustration of the psychology of two elderly French intellectuals.

This is where the phenomenon of 'mauvaise foi' takes on its full importance. Because André recognizes the limitations imposed by the ageing process, he has slipped into ways of thinking about himself and his future that he comes to regard as self-indulgent, and at the end he decides to renew himself by taking a different direction (**83**). Madame, however, is seen as both unrealistic and given to self-deception in relation to ageing. Indeed, her refusal to accept that time passes, that bodies, relationships and circumstances change, is presented as the underlying reason for all her particular problems. In an important sequence just after she rejoins André in the final section (and where she shuts herself away in the dark, rather as Laurence does), she not only sees through her 'mauvaise foi' in each of the key areas, but also draws them together in this way:

> J'avais dit à André: «Je ne vois pas ce qu'on perd à vieillir.» Eh bien! maintenant, je voyais. J'ai toujours refusé d'envisager la vie à la manière de Fitzgerald comme «un processus de dégradation». Je pensais que mes rapports avec André ne s'altéreraient jamais, que mon œuvre ne cesserait pas de s'enrichir, que Philippe ressemblerait chaque jour davantage à l'homme que j'avais voulu faire de lui. Mon corps, je ne m'en inquiétais pas. Et je croyais que même le silence portait des fruits. Quelle illusion!(**71**)

The final reconciliation with André relieves a little of the gloom that Madame feels at this point, but it involves no going back on her new recognition that ageing is an inescapable reality. And no going back on the firm awareness that time passes, for the fleeting 'impression d'éternité' that she experiences is seen for what it is: 'un instant le temps s'était arrêté. Il allait se remettre à couler' (**83-84**).

There is no trace of facile optimism at the end of 'L'Âge de discrétion' and one of its major strengths consists in portraying the mental twists and turns of a woman who never entirely abandons her love of the truth, but fights a considerable battle with self-deception. The story is also convincing, on the whole, in its depiction of the

bumpy but touching relationship between Madame and André, and of
the intense, fragile link between Madame and her son. There is—in
different measures—enough consistence in the characters of André,
Philippe and even the objectionable Irène (who could easily belong to
the social set of Les Belles Images) for them to fulfil their functions
in the story quite well. André's mother, Manette, is a wholly
undeveloped figure, but brings a little colour to the tale by her very
eccentricity. On the other hand, Madame's teacher friend, Martine, is
a rather flat character and acts as a vehicle for certain minor
elements in a rather predictable way.

   Through none of these characters does the outside world impinge
to any significant extent upon what is essentially a private or
domestic story. When Madame herself refers, for instance, to
building developments in Paris or technological advances, she
characteristically does so with a certain bewilderment (11; 13; 17).
She has a social conscience, but her own commitment to the political
causes to which André devotes so much time (16) seems less than
wholehearted. Her one outburst against the bourgeoisie stands out as
exceptional, but is in itself quite revealing: 'Ces gros bourgeois
pourris de fric, influents, importants me semblent encore plus
détestables que le milieu frivole et mondain contre lequel ma
jeunesse s'est insurgée'(30). It reinforces suggestions elsewhere in
the story that both André and Madame have been left somewhat
stranded by social and political developments. She speaks of the
Algerian War as 'cette guerre qui nous avait ravagés et qui semblait
maintenant n'avoir jamais eu lieu'(33) and André acknowledges that
now '«pratiquement aucune cause n'est tout à fait la nôtre»'(78).
Near the end he recognizes the importance of doing everything
possible to reduce human suffering (77), yet his final decision to
learn new things '«juste pour les savoir»'(83) hardly seems
calculated to help. Perhaps the rapid changes in the outside world
registered rather faintly in the story represent one more aspect of the
passage of time to which older people have difficulty in adjusting.

   If the narrative of 'L'Âge de discrétion' does not have a strong
political or social setting, it does have a broadly literary orientation
that is entirely appropriate when the narrator is portrayed as a
writer and literary critic. This is not simply a matter of the
numerous literary allusions and the quotations that sprinkle the text,
for the style itself has certain minor poetic qualities not entirely
common in Beauvoir's fiction. Madame is not only sensitive to sights
and smells, but also inclined to relate them to memories of her past,
in a way that often gives resonance to her descriptions and
occasionally produces memorable turns of phrase. These qualities are

perhaps most in evidence in the early part of the story, when Madame's state of mind is one of excitement, but later in the text even her unpleasant discoveries and her depression are conveyed to us in telling images and carefully chosen words. This is all entirely in keeping with a character who regards literature as a very special activity. It also raises the question of the general character of the narrative, which has to be read as something resembling a diary written by Madame. Yet it is no ordinary kind of diary, since, although the first two sections of the text correspond to two specific moments of narration not much more than twelve hours apart, the whole of the rest of the story (covering more than three weeks) appears to be related from the same narrative moment, for the narrative present tense does not return until the last few lines of all. This may cause the reader to ask some unanswered, and perhaps unanswerable, questions about the status of the narrative. And on the formal level it means that, rather oddly, the divisions between sections three and four and between sections four and five are different in kind from the first two divisions, deriving from convenient breaks in the events of the story rather than from narrative moments.

If this is an untidy feature of the story, the reader may well feel that in other respects 'L'Âge de discrétion' is over-systematic, even programmatic, in a way that rules out the open-ended quality displayed by the most stimulating fiction. The fact that Madame lists all of her major problems early on, claiming that they are solved (**16**), then lists them again later, indicating that they are unresolved after all (**71**) is somewhat wooden, though of little significance in itself. But Beauvoir's attempt to draw all of those problems tightly together and present them as undergoing exactly the same phased development is less than wholly successful. That ageing is at the root of the rift between Madame and Philippe as well as the one between herself and André is already only true in a very vague sense. That the timing of these rifts actually coincides with any particular revelations about her own body is less than clear. And that her latest book should appear and be poorly received at precisely the time when the other issues come to a head is a little difficult to accept. Matters are made worse by the fact that these features are not implicit in the story but deliberately spelled out for us by the narrator. If there is some general principle whereby a reader cherishes most, in fiction, that which s/he has had to find or work for, rather than that which is directly given, then 'L'Âge de discrétion' will not prove an especially rewarding story. Beauvoir herself came to be disappointed with it: 'De mes trois récits, c'est celui qui me satisfait le moins. Il n'est pas construit à travers des silences: il est écrit en clair, selon mon ancienne technique' (*TCF*, 176-7). Certainly, it makes fewer demands on the reader's participation than the two subsequent stories in the collection.

'Monologue'

As is the case in *Les Belles Images*, 'Monologue', the second of the stories in *La Femme rompue*, plunges us abruptly into the world and mentality of the central character, Murielle; but here the device immediately generates a certain hostility as well as some confusion. Obviously incomplete punctuation in the written text and an unexpected crudeness of language (the first phrase of the story is 'Les cons!'—**87**), combined with the thoroughly unhelpful manner of introducing proper names and other references, initially leave us disoriented, even assaulted:

> Ils se gavent de mauvais foie gras et de dinde brûlée ils s'en pourlèchent Albert et Madame Nanard Étiennette leurs chiards ma mère; c'est contre nature que mon propre frère ma propre mère me préfèrent mon ex-mari. Je n'en ai rien à foutre d'eux seulement qu'ils ne m'empêchent pas de dormir. (**88**)

We soon come to accept these factors as appropriate to what is presented as the private monologue of an unhinged and vindictive woman. Nevertheless, two major tasks continue to require a specific effort on the reader's part: establishing the setting and circumstances of the monologue; and reconstructing enough of Murielle's past to make sense of the references and details that come pouring out.

The latter task, which has something of the fascination of a puzzle, is not especially difficult. There are few obfuscations as such (even the first reference to Murielle's younger brother as 'Madame Nanard', though misleading, has its point, since she claims he is a homosexual); there are only minor loose ends (the single reference to 'Olivier' is never explained or developed—**90**); and although Murielle does not mention events in her past in strict chronological order, neither is that order entirely flouted or distorted in an eccentric way, so that there is a broadly sequential flow to her references. All of this is important, for the relative clarity of the basic 'facts' about Murielle's past enables the reader simply to register the framework and concentrate on the more complicated business of deciding whether certain other details should be seen as facts, or as inventions on Murielle's part. Only in this way can a general judgement be formed on Murielle herself. It is worthwhile recording, therefore, what can uncontroversially be taken as the main elements of Murielle's past, if only because they bring into focus the claims that we have reason to be more doubtful about.

Murielle, who is forty-three, was always fonder of her father than her mother, but the latter had to take full charge of her upbringing when the father died. Murielle was probably jealous of her younger brother Nanard, but kept in contact with him even after he married Étiennette. Apparently with the encouragement of her mother, she married her first husband, Albert, when they were both quite young. She was about twenty-one when their daughter Sylvie was born. The quarrels between Murielle and Albert led to a divorce, whereby Sylvie continued to live with her mother but saw Albert regularly. Murielle then had an affair with Florent, but broke it off in order to marry Tristan, a banker of forty-five, by whom she had a son, Francis, when she was thirty-two. Particularly after Tristan left her four years later, taking Francis with him, Murielle had problems in bringing up her daughter on her own. She was unhappy about Sylvie's continuing relationship with both Albert and Tristan. There was a major incident when Murielle read a private diary and went to talk to her teacher about it, for Sylvie learned what had happened, was furious, and stopped keeping her diary for the last two years of her life. At one point, she ran off to be with Albert, but Murielle called in the police to bring her back. When Sylvie committed suicide, at the age of seventeen, by an overdose of drugs, she left a note for her father ('«Papa je te demande pardon mais je n'en peux plus»'—113), which Murielle tore up. All those who knew Sylvie apparently considered that Murielle was to blame, her mother publicly accusing her of being responsible; she lost weight and became ill. Murielle's mother and other family have had very little contact with her since Sylvie's death, which took place five years ago. She sees Tristan and Francis regularly and is desperately trying to persuade Tristan that they should both come back to live with her, but he has been resisting this suggestion.

At the time when the monologue is delivered, Murielle is expecting a visit from Tristan and Francis the following day, and this brings us on to another category of 'facts' that can uncontroversially be drawn from the tortured, self-subverting text. These relate to the setting and circumstances of the monologue, as well as to such minor events as it incorporates. The time is New Year's Eve, which is significant in a number of respects. Traditionally a time for gatherings of families and friends, this is when people almost have a right to hold parties and make noise. But, consequently, it is also a time when those who are alone are likely to be made particularly conscious of their solitude and loneliness. Murielle is, of course, alone in her flat (scarcely prepared to leave her armchair), aware of parties going on around her, but also conjuring up in her mind the similar activities that members of her family will be engaged in elsewhere. She would dearly like her family to make contact with her, but is so sure that they will not that she has blocked the telephone bell with earplugs ('boules Quiès'), in order not to hear it failing to ring (**87**).

Her whole monologue is punctuated by allusions to the sound and movement around her. Sometimes her imagination runs riot as she interprets—usually in terms of depraved sexual practices—the activities of the merrymakers. Yet we have no reason to question the general grid of references within which her own thoughts and feelings are expressed. Such references show the world periodically breaking into Murielle's train of thoughts, but the 'interruptions' themselves generate further thoughts and memories. We must presume that a period of a few hours is involved, for Murielle records: the noisy arrival of the partygoers (**87**); the midnight celebrations and dancing (**90**); antics in the street (**95**); a rather odd brief period of strong wind (**100-1**); the end of the dancing (**104**); the departure of the guests (**108**); and the eventual deathly silence in the flats and in the street (**111**).

This is the background of activity against which the monologue is delivered, but in the course of it Murielle herself carries out only three significant actions. At the height of the festivities around her she tries telephoning Tristan, but receives no reply (**99**). She later telephones her mother, who rings off very abruptly (**105**). Then in the early hours, when all is quiet around her, she rings Tristan once more, waking him up and launching into a long diatribe that causes him to hang up and refuse to answer the phone again (**114-7**). This last call, which comes at the end of the story (and is separated off from the rest of the monologue by the only gap in the text), is of particular importance in a number of ways. Firstly, it gives us a point of reference outside the monologue proper, in that we can see that Murielle talks to others in her life in exactly the manner that she 'talks to herself'. Secondly, it is her only action having any real effect in the story, and that effect, significantly, is the opposite of what she intends, since it appears to leave Tristan even more determined than ever not to live with her again (**117**). And, thirdly, this in turn leaves Murielle even more isolated and lonely than she was at the beginning, when her one hope was the return of Tristan and Francis. New Year's Eve is the time for new beginnings, but the end of 'Monologue' makes it clear that there will be none for Murielle. This is an unusual story within the body of Beauvoir's fiction for many reasons, but not least because it closes the door on all possible development. Any future improvement in Murielle's situation seems to have been ruled out.

In fact, the very core of the story lies in its presentation of a character who is incapable of learning or adjusting her behaviour in any way. This is not a matter of intelligence as such, but once more a question of self-deception. In this respect, Beauvoir's account of the origins of the story is revealing:

> Dans le *Monologue* il s'agit aussi du rapport de la vérité avec les mensonges du discours: certaines lettres que j'avais reçues m'avaient montré comment elle pouvait éclater à travers des phrases destinées à la dissimuler. [...] J'ai choisi un cas extrême: une femme qui se sait responsable du suicide de sa fille et que tout son entourage condamne. J'ai essayé de construire l'ensemble des sophismes, des vaticinations, des fuites par lesquels elle tente de se donner raison. (*TCF*, 176)

Beauvoir presumably needed to assess to what extent her women correspondents were trying to deceive her and to what extent themselves, but it was the latter phenomenon that intrigued her. Hence a major feature of the very form of 'Monologue' is that, since Murielle is talking only to herself, there can be no question (until the very end) of her lying to anyone other than herself: any discrepancy between her 'discours' and what we regard as 'vérité' can only be attributable to 'mauvaise foi'.

Beauvoir emphasizes Murielle's attitude towards her daughter and this is, indeed, the most consequential area in which her character's self-deception is shown to operate. It is clear from the 'facts' summarized above that there was a great deal to condemn in Murielle's upbringing of Sylvie. There is also a reference to her attitude to her daughter's friendships that constitutes a kind of inversion of the treatment of this theme in *Les Belles Images,* for Murielle tried to force a particular friend upon Sylvie and punished her when she found the girl boring (**103**). In fact, Murielle can be seen to exemplify, in an extreme and blameworthy form, all of the errors in upbringing committed or nearly committed by the mothers in *Les Belles Images* and 'L'Âge de discrétion'. The recurrent refrain in 'Monologue' is that children should be brought up 'properly', which clearly implies, for Murielle, not just a strong measure of control (her analogy with training maidservants is revealing—**92**), but also minimum inconvenience for the parents. She thinks at one point of women who are lucky enough to have children 'pour les servir' (**93**), but what reveals even more starkly her seriously defective attitudes as a parent is her treatment of her son, Francis. She argues that a son needs his mother only because she wants Tristan to come back and care for her. Her real degree of concern for her son's welfare may best be gauged from her threat to commit suicide in front of him, or even to kill him too (**97**; **117**). And in the face of her daughter's real suicide, Murielle's reaction is to feel sorry for herself: 'Sylvie Sylvie pourquoi m'as-tu fait ça!' (**111**; cf. **104**).

In the light of all of this, Murielle's repeated claim that she has been a perfect mother (**108**), together with more specific claims about how well she has treated her children, can be seen as gross self-deception. Her assertion that she was always tender towards Sylvie, who was a particularly ungrateful girl (**94**; **97**), rings hollow; and her belief that Sylvie would have been grateful in the end is only a conveniently unverifiable supposition. If we feel reluctant to go as far as Beauvoir when she says that Murielle knows that she was responsible for her daughter's suicide, then we must remember that seeing the character as shot through with self-deception necessarily involves believing that there are a range of things that she is actually aware of, but is trying to hide from herself.

After all, in less complex areas of Murielle's life and character her 'mauvaise foi' is evident enough. She tries to persuade herself that she has always been indifferent to money (**95**), but her monologue betrays that she has been acutely conscious of its presence or absence in every major relationship that she has entered into (**96**; **106-7**; **117**). Her belief that she is no longer remotely interested in sex (**105**) is another unmistakeable example of self-deception, for she is seen to be obsessed with the sexual activities of others to a thoroughly unhealthy degree (**89**; **91**; **105**). In fact, Murielle deludes herself on almost every count in her view of her own conduct, her own character. She even accuses everyone else of self-deception and persuades herself that she is characterized by frankness, lucidity and integrity: 'Les gens n'acceptent pas qu'on leur dise leurs vérités. [...] Moi je suis lucide je suis franche j'arrache les masques' (**102**).

It is obvious by this stage, even if we have forgotten the occasional ravings in the monologue and the fact that at the end Murielle bangs her head against the wall so hard that it bleeds (**118**), that the text deals with such an extreme case of self-deception that it takes us into the territory of mental illness. Beauvoir claims that

Murielle's distortion of reality is carried to the point of 'paraphrénie', a general term of psychopathology covering both paranoia and schizophrenia (*TCF*, 176). In order to challenge others' judgement of her, Murielle is obliged to hate the whole world. Thus we see her, for instance, distressed to breathe in air that has already been breathed by others and, at the very end, harassing (a non-existent) God in the way that she harasses those around her: 'Vous me devez cette revanche mon Dieu. J'exige que vous me la donniez' (**118**). These excesses give rise to some difficult questions regarding our reaction to the text. Reading it involves dealing with an alien mentality, and the barrier formed by Murielle's crude language, her weird imagination, her vile images, will be one that some readers have the greatest difficulty in surmounting. Assuming, however, that we pass through this barrier to the extent of recognizing that Murielle is mentally ill, what consequences follow for our general attitude towards the character and her monologue? Presumably we must now be prepared to exercise more sympathy towards Murielle than an initial, cool analysis of discrepancies between 'discours' and 'vérité' implies. Indeed, it is inconceivable that Beauvoir, even though she does not mention this in her comments, should have wished to portray such a sick mind, such a pathetic, isolated character, without evoking sympathy on her behalf. We have to acknowledge that Murielle's self-deception is intimately bound up with her mental illness, and recognize that it has harmed her as well as others. And we must at least consider the possibility that the harm that she has done to others is in some sense excusable. Yet it is not clear how far the implications of this must go.

It would be foolish to be categorical or prescriptive, but one or two guidelines can be discerned and may help individual readers to find their own way through other complexities in the story. For one thing, a recognition that Murielle is mentally ill is likely to change our attitude not only to her 'mauvaise foi', but also to some other objectionable attitudes that she displays. The sheer cruelty of her observations on, for instance, other races and nationalities ('je m'en branle des Bicots des Juifs des Nègres'—**102**), or on the victims of violence ('Un million d'enfants massacrés et après?'—**102-3**), must now be seen in a rather different light. How seriously can we take these attitudes? Should we not suppose that another aspect of Murielle's self-deception consists in persuading herself that she can possibly hold such appalling views? There are curious echoes of *Les Belles Images* here. Murielle looks as cruel as Laurence is sensitive, yet some of the things that she objects to are the targets of

Laurence's anxiety as well; a few of her comments could come from Laurence herself. Both are concerned about population levels and unimpressed by technological advances (92), and Murielle is equally scathing about facile optimism (102). To whatever extent they are a product of self-deception, then, Murielle's expressed views are sometimes a complex mixture of nonsense and insight.

The reference to *Les Belles Images,* moreover, may provide us with another pointer to the degree of sympathy that we should feel for Murielle. Her presentation of her mother and other family in 'Monologue' is bitter and brutal. But it might usefully be seen as an extreme development of the detachment and harshness that Laurence herself sometimes displays in describing her mother and husband. The point can even be taken a little further if we return to the theme of upbringing. Once more a direct reaction against her own upbringing is suggested as a factor in the way in which Murielle brought up her own children. Of course, we may doubt her claims that her mother struck her (88), and neglected or abandoned her (97; 99; 103; 112), but these particular claims do not look as questionable as many others made by Murielle about her mother. And, however this may be, the references at least have the merit of reminding us that we must assume that Murielle had some kind of upbringing. This is important because it is an unavoidable direction in which to look when we begin considering the origins of Murielle's mental illness. If Laurence's mental instability arose from circumstances in which she loved her father but was dominated and brought up by her mother, is it not plausible to relate Murielle's more extreme mental problems to an upbringing of exactly the same kind?

Clearly speculation of this sort can scarcely be carried further on the basis of the text of "Monologue', but it is worth noticing, finally, that the pattern of argument just used is perfectly generalizable. In the end we must ask a broad question that cannot be answered: What core of 'truth' lies behind Murielle's paranoia? The question is unanswerable because the form and nature of the story are such as to give us only the most slender textual evidence against which to check any hypothesis on this issue. One might think that Murielle's mother hangs up on her rather quickly, especially for New Year's Eve, but it is difficult to find hard evidence on the basis of which to take the argument further. The last word about 'Monologue' may be that both its strength and its limits lie in its monologue form: it is a powerful and successful attempt to project us into the strange mentality of a tortured woman, but its very nature gives the reader minimal help in taking any kind of grip on the case or making any kind of sensible judgement. Our eventual attitude towards Murielle may derive as much from other, extraneous sources as from the text itself. In this respect, the fact that the story belongs to a collection, as well as to a body of work by a particular author, is perhaps of unusual importance to the process of interpretation.

'La Femme rompue'

'La Femme rompue', the final story in the collection of the same name, is by far the longest, being nearly twice the length of 'L'Âge de discrétion' and four times as long as "Monologue". Its central plot as such, however, is the simple and commonplace one of a marital breakdown.

Monique Lacombe, who is forty-four, was married to Maurice in 1944 and has been his wife for twenty-two years. They were medical students together and married when Monique became pregnant. At that stage Maurice gave up any ambition of becoming a hospital doctor and took up a post as a general practitioner with the car firm of Simca. Ten years before the events of the story, against the advice of Monique, he accepted the offer of carrying out more specialized work, including research, as part of a team in a 'polyclinique'. The fact of Monique's strong opposition to this move, together with her subsequent failure to take great interest in Maurice's progress, was at least one major factor behind a change in his feelings towards her. About two years later he began having affairs with other women and eventually, some eighteen months before the events of the story, began a serious liaison with Noëllie Guérard, a successful, divorced lawyer of thirty-eight He had kept this affair, like the earlier ones, from Monique, and continues to lie to her about its duration after he first tells her about it. Stage by stage in the story itself she learns how serious the relationship is and has been. As Maurice comes to devote more and more time to Noëllie, Monique becomes increasingly distraught, developing some physical symptoms, and finally sees a psychiatrist. By this time Maurice has signalled his intention of leaving the family home, ostensibly to live on his own for a time. Near the end of the text, when he is preparing to leave, Monique visits her younger daughter in New York, to see what light she can cast on the family's past. She instructs him not to meet her at the airport on her return and fearfully faces the future alone.

No one reading this résumé would be surprised to learn that the story was serialized in the women's magazine *Elle* in the autumn of

1967, although those knowing Beauvoir's work might be puzzled by her motives for allowing this. (In fact, she needed the money and also wanted a wide audience for the engraved illustrations by her sister Hélène). In any case, Beauvoir regarded the reactions of many women readers who wrote to her—'je fus submergée de lettres émanant de femmes rompues, demi rompues, ou en instance de rupture'(*TCF,* 177)—as profoundly mistaken: 'elles partageaient l'aveuglement de Monique. Leurs réactions reposaient sur un énorme contresens'(*ibid.,* p. 178). However aware one may be, therefore, of the dangers of centring literary criticism on accounts of authors' intentions, it is difficult not to begin discussion of 'La Femme rompue' by referring to what Beauvoir claims to have had in mind in writing the story:

> Il ne s'agissait pas pour moi de raconter en clair cette banale histoire mais de montrer, à travers son journal intime, comment la victime essayait d'en fuir la vérité. La difficulté était encore plus grande que dans *Les Belles Images* car Laurence cherche timidement la lumière tandis que tout l'effort de Monique tend à l'oblitérer, par des mensonges à soi, des oublis, des erreurs; de page en page le journal se conteste: mais à travers de nouvelles fabulations, de nouvelles omissions. Elle tisse elle-même les ténèbres dans lesquelles elle sombre au point de perdre sa propre image. J'aurais voulu que le lecteur lût ce récit comme un roman policier; j'ai semé de-ci de-là des indices qui permettent de trouver la clé du mystère: mais à condition qu'on dépiste Monique comme on dépiste un coupable. (*TCF,* 175-6)

Much hinges, then, on the fact that the story is again focalized wholly through the central female character. Indeed, the narrative situation here is clearer than in all of the previous stories examined, since 'La Femme rompue' is presented strictly in the guise of Monique's diary. In purely formal terms, there is little that is remarkable about the nature and structure of the diary. Monique occasionally writes more than once on the same day, but, in a diary of eighty-five entries covering some six and a half months, only for brief periods does she make entries on a daily basis. It is plausible, for instance, that she should be shown as writing on eight successive days at the time of Maurice's first revelation of his affair (**127-42**); and that this particular run of entries should include both the shortest ('Ainsi c'est arrivé. Ça m'est arrivé'—**130**) and the longest (the following day) in the whole diary. Similarly, gaps of three days or more between entries are common, but the only two much longer gaps are explained by Monique, who consciously, if temporarily, broke off writing the diary altogether (**223; 239**). Entries are made significantly less frequently in the last stages of the story and this, too, can be seen to derive from the nature of events. The great majority of entries are, in fact, fairly short (characteristically, between one and two pages), so that the general effect is that of a long succession of snapshots of Monique's gradually deteriorating state of mind. In short, the diary form, in sharp contrast to the monologue of the preceding story, is perfectly adapted to the portrayal of a character whose situation and patterns of thought and behaviour are changing.

Yet Beauvoir's crucial point about the extent of Monique's endeavours to hide from herself the truth about these changes is easy to verify, for by following the successive entries of the diary the reader is able to watch her in the very process of trying to construct procedures for her own self-deception, even if, in most cases, events finally force her to acknowledge reality. Monique's initial response to the revelation of Maurice's liaison with Noëllie is to regard the affair as a sexual whim on Maurice's part ('une histoire de peau'— 137). But immediately afterwards she acknowledges that 'à l'âge de Maurice ça compte, une histoire de peau'(140) and that Noëllie is more likely to be sexually skilled than frigid (141). Moreover, Monique soon goes back on her earlier implication that all is well in her own sexual relations with Maurice, now referring to his 'tiédeur' (141). Later still, she talks to a friend as if this has long constituted a problem (196), one for which she even feels obliged to take some responsibility: 'Au lieu de ranimer notre vie sexuelle, je me fascinais sur les souvenirs de nos anciennes nuits'(211).

However, sexuality is only one area in which she tries to deceive herself as her general view of Maurice's affair is obliged to change. She has to abandon her original idea of Noëllie as someone playing games and consider her as a rival (148). Having rejected the possibility that Noëllie could have any influence over Maurice, she is forced to entertain it (153). Having convinced herself that she will always come first for Maurice, she is forced to contemplate the idea that Maurice may prefer Noëllie (168). But still she clings to the idea that he loves her, telling Maurice that he is simply sacrificing his love to his vanity (186). Even after Maurice announces (admittedly in a moment of anger) that he stopped loving her nearly ten years earlier (187), she refuses to accept this entirely. Very late on she can still tell her friend Isabelle: '«Au fond Maurice n'a jamais cessé de m'aimer»' (228). And when she considers going to New York to talk to Lucienne, it is in order to restore her old relationship with him (236).

Yet if all of this is based on the premiss that news of Maurice's affair with Noëllie came as a bombshell to Monique, we can also go back and question that assumption. In fact, she soon begins recording feelings she had even before his confession that Maurice had changed (**141**), and she eventually acknowledges that 'Ce n'est pas tout à fait au hasard que j'ai posé la question: Il y a une femme dans ta vie?' (**171**). We see, too, at this point that there has been self-deception in her various accounts of the parting from Maurice at Nice aerodrome with which the diary begins. At first she records that they were both moved by the leave-taking (**122**). Then she admits that the holiday they had just spent together had been dismal (**128**). And finally she admits that Maurice's 'anxiété' when they parted was some kind of guilt about Noëllie, suggesting that she had almost guessed what was wrong at the time (**171**).

In observing Monique's 'mauvaise foi' in relation to Maurice's affair, we are driven back in time and simultaneously find ourselves unravelling aspects of her past with Maurice. As in each of the stories already examined, it becomes apparent that an integral part of the reading process is a certain reconstruction of events that took place before the events of the story proper. And in this, the 'help' forthcoming from the narrator, although it is all that we have, is of very mixed quality! This is to say that Monique's self-deception is seen to extend back in the most serious fashion over most, or all, of the twenty-two years of her marriage. Discovering the details of this, in fact, constitutes a significant part of the detective work that the reader needs to carry out. And whatever the minutiae of the process may be, the establishing of a clear schematic framework is indispensable to a full appreciation of the story.

Working backwards stage by stage from the period of time covered by the diary, one can show that, for every step, there is strong evidence that Monique has deceived herself in her past and about her past. In the story itself we see her not only abandoning a job that she takes up on the psychiatrist's advice (**241**), but also turning down Maurice's earlier offer to find her a post (**206**). This raises the question of why she has never pursued a career of her own (which Beauvoir implies is an important element in the story), and we soon notice discrepancies in Monique's explanations. Was it the desire to be utterly available for her children (**125**), but a kind of sacrifice on her part?(**194**) Was it that she found herself unable to face the realities of her chosen medical profession?(**195**) Has she forgotten particular proposals for work that Maurice previously put to her because accepting them would have taken a courage that she lacked?(**197**) Is her reason for not starting work now really that she wants more time to herself and time with Maurice?(**123**) It is hard to believe that all of her comments can be drawn together in a consistent stance. The strong suggestion is that her justification of 'la vocation du foyer' is a rationalization (to herself) of certain underlying anxieties or weaknesses.

It relates, too, to the matter of Maurice's change of job ten years earlier, which we learn, as the diary progresses, to have been crucial. Beneath all the different claims and counter-claims concerning Maurice's reasons and the appropriateness of the move lies the issue of Monique's 'participation' in his earlier work at Simca. The precise nature of this participation is registered early on (**138**), but only later does it emerge exactly how important it was for Monique: 'Ce lien entre nous, si important pour moi, il a choisi de le briser' (**192**). At this point we realize that it was for selfish reasons, rather than in Maurice's interests, that she opposed the move. There is a further hint that her complete failure to keep up with his work thereafter sprang, not from its specialized nature, but from her misguided attempt to 'punish' Maurice for changing jobs.

Even this major incident, however, can only be fully understood against the background of the early years, and even the moment, of their marriage. On the question of the pregnancy that precipitated the marriage, Monique's claims that they were 'tous deux responsables', that they both agreed to have the child, and that Maurice had his own reasons for not wanting to go on being a hospital houseman (**159**), look illusory when she lets slip that she put too much faith in the calendar (**212**), and above all when Maurice accuses her of making him leave hospital work (**186**). Maurice later takes back his accusation (**207**), but we remain tempted by Marie Lambert's whole picture of the marriage, which is less convoluted than Monique alleges: 'pour ne pas s'avouer ses regrets, Maurice a misé sur l'amour, il a voulu le bonheur avec frénésie; une fois celle-ci tombée, il a retrouvé la rancune qu'il avait refoulée'(**212**). Monique is right to argue that the explanation works only if there have been subsequent signs of resentment on Maurice's part, but when she admits that she has indeed noticed such signs, then in a general way we feel that the circle is complete. We now broadly understand both what has happened in the marriage as a whole and the way in which Monique's complex self-deceiving strategies, though not entirely the cause of the disaster, have certainly made matters worse in a variety of ways.

Chronologically, there is one more factor behind all of the stages of Monique's past just examined, although it does not in itself constitute another example of her 'mauvaise foi', much less offer an explanation of it. This factor is the now familiar one of Monique's

upbringing, or at least her relations with her parents. There are no
substantive references to her mother in the diary, but we would be
unwise to ignore what she writes about her father. It seems likely
that she studied medicine because of her admiration for her father
('La médecine, telle que papa l'exerçait dans son cabinet de Bagnolet,
je pensais qu'il n'y avait pas de plus beau métier'—**195**), and this
may well be the profound reason why, when she found herself
unable to take up the profession, she was so happy to be involved
with Maurice's patients and so opposed to his taking up a post that
would preclude this (**138**). When she sees a psychiatrist, he
(predictably) wants her to talk about her parents (**239**), but even
before this Monique has admitted that her father's death may have
been an especially important moment for her: 'J'ai arrêté le temps à
partir de ce moment-là' (**211**). Insofar as she is right to see all of her
problems as linked with her inability to acknowledge the passage of
time (**211**), this may be a particularly significant observation. In any
case, we are able to see that Monique's multi-layered self-deception
relates right back to a family situation in which she adored her father.

By now we are in a strong position to confirm Beauvoir's remark
that 'Aucune phrase n'a en soi son sens, aucun détail n'a de valeur
sinon replacé dans l'ensemble du journal' (*TCF*, 176), but it would be
a bad mistake to believe that Monique is never aware of this aspect of
her diary, for she does of course make some comments on the diary
itself while writing it. It is true that her various accounts of her
motives for starting and continuing the diary (which correspond to
the different stages of her acknowledgement of the true state of
affairs when she and Maurice parted in Nice) offer another example
of self-deception. She first says that she began writing the diary out
of joy, for her own sake (**122**), then that it was because solitude
disconcerted her (**139**), or as an attempt to ward off anxiety (**221**).
In reaffirming this last view, moreover, she acknowledges the
discrepancy between her earlier statements (**222**). But this
acknowledgement is, in its way, as typical of the diary as is the
attempted self-deception itself. In a series of earlier asides and
isolated comments, Monique has drawn attention to the sort of
omissions that her diary contains (**128**); hinted that she is prepared to
lie (**134**); and noted the obvious fact that her memory is sometimes
defective (**185**). She has even alluded to a mental process whereby
she suppresses or 'neutralizes' memories (**190**), and suggested that
she has 'déformé les faits' (**213**). All of this corroborates, detail by
detail, Beauvoir's list of procedures whereby Monique tries to escape
the truth. And then, near the end, the character openly admits that
her diary has been one long record of delusion and self-deception: 'Il

n'y a pas une ligne de ce journal qui n'appelle une correction ou un démenti'(**222**). Her account of events and her honesty with herself in the diary could scarcely be more seriously discredited, and it is small wonder that Monique soon begins to break down and stops writing for a while.

Nevertheless, the most important point to note is that it is Monique herself who recognizes the self-deception and discredits the diary. Not only is there no trace at all of this point in Beauvoir's comments, it actually undermines one of her claims, and even possibly the general thrust of her argument. It is quite visibly not the case that all of Monique's energy goes into fleeing from the truth. 'La Femme rompue' would be a drastically different story if Monique did not have moments of lucidity and honesty. Admittedly, many such moments are indeed succeeded by 'de nouvelles fabulations, de nouvelles omissions'(*TCF,* 175), but the fact remains that, for each of the examples of 'mauvaise foi' examined, passages are to be found where Monique acknowledges the fact of her earlier self-deception quite explicitly. At the most general level, her harsh comments on her diary are an instance of this, as is her admission that she has systematically deceived herself about Maurice and Noëllie: 'Je me mentais. Comme je me suis menti!'(223).

At the more detailed level, quite apart from the moments of lucidity already mentioned, there are occasions when she sees almost at once that she is on the point of deceiving herself and pulls herself up (**155**; **174-5**; **207-8**); when she recognizes that her image of herself has been 'trop flatteuse peut-être' (**180**); when she accurately notes that she does not adopt certain methods of blinking facts favoured by others (**173**); when she acknowledges that her new-found interest in culture is no more than 'un alibi'(**183**); when she is really rather remarkably clear-headed and honest about her own 'unique flirt' with Quillan (**136-7**; **168-70**); and when she accepts that she has been a victim of the 'aveuglement' that has so astonished her in other women (**194**). None of this refutes the point that Monique is a self-deceiver. It is even consistent with Beauvoir's comment that 'La vérité n'est jamais avouée' (*TCF,* 176), provided that we take this to mean that Monique never puts all of the elements of her earlier self-deception together to make the kind of picture that it is possible for the reader to make. But it does show that, far from being shot through with self-deception, Monique is a fairly complex mixture of 'mauvaise foi' and lucidity. The point receives further confirmation if we remember the considerable number of occasions in the diary when she acknowledges faults in her own character other than the tendency to delude herself: impatience, intransigence, lack of self-control, awkwardness, emotional blackmail, and so on. Monique is wholly unlike Murielle, who is utterly unable to admit to any faults and whose self-deception carries her deeply into mental illness.

It seems that Beauvoir rather lost sight of this in making her comments in *Tout compte fait,* presumably because of her surprise that so many readers had failed to see the importance of Monique's self-deception. It is strange, for instance, that the comments take so little account of the fact that Monique has two grown-up children, Colette and Lucienne. As we would expect by now, 'La Femme rompue' gives considerable prominence to the matter of the upbringing of the two daughters. There is little question here of the mother continuing to try to force particular values upon an adult child ('L'Âge de discrétion'), or tyrannizing and manipulating younger children ('Monologue'). Nor is there detailed scrutiny of the early stages of upbringing (*Les Belles Images*). The emphasis in 'La Femme rompue' falls to a large extent upon the matter of how successful Monique has been in bringing up her daughters.

The younger daughter, Lucienne, left home for America less than a year before the beginning of the diary, and this natural watershed accentuates the way in which Maurice's affair brings into question the whole of Monique's past, so that from early on she is asking herself questions about how her daughters have turned out. Then, in a moment of anger, Maurice focuses these questions by accusing her of pushing Colette into 'un mariage idiot' and driving Lucienne away from home (**186**). This charge hurts Monique almost more than any other ('Si j'ai manqué l'éducation de mes filles, toute ma vie n'est qu'un échec'—**213-4**), and a very great deal hinges, for Monique and the reader alike, on whether the accusation is seen as justified. It is no more than another version of the same question to ask whether her view of the children's upbringing is simply another area in which her self-deception has operated.

One of the interesting and distinctive features of the treatment of the theme of upbringing in 'La Femme rompue' is the fact that the two daughters develop in such different directions. Hence many of the references in the story involve drawing a sharp contrast between them (**122; 129; 162; 188**). Monique acknowledges that she had difficulties in bringing up Lucienne, and even experienced some hostility, but she made a great effort to leave both daughters free and her general view early on is that this has been entirely successful (**162**). What is perfectly clear is that, by the end of the story, the doubts sown by Maurice's defection and by his explicit charges have caused her to change her view of both daughters. She finally sees Colette as rather conformist, lacking in initiative, and leading a narrow, dull life (**219**); and Lucienne as rather lonely and embittered, less sure of herself than she had thought (**248-50**). Yet it is by no means clear that this amounts to saying that Monique has fundamentally deceived herself about her daughters. She is strikingly clear-headed about the purely personal pleasure that she has gained from having them ('une forme d'égoïsme'—**143**), and perhaps the worst that one can say is that there has been a certain wishful thinking in her view of how happy they are.

Once again, the form of the story is such that, in order to form a sound judgement on the matter, we need to make a conscious effort to remind ourselves of Maurice's part in the upbringing of the girls. Firstly, we must remember that Monique's desire to have Maurice practise medicine in the way that her father did is intriguingly echoed in Maurice's expectations for his daughters. He wanted Colette to continue her scientific studies (**161**), and he was even hoping that Lucienne would go on to work with him (**162**). In other words, in considering Maurice's view of their daughters and of Monique's 'success' with them, we must allow for a level of disappointment that they have not turned out as he had hoped. Against the feeling that Colette simply followed her mother's example, we must set Maurice's resentment that she did not follow his (**157**); and against his suggestion that Monique was so oppressive that she drove Lucienne away, we must set the possibility that his own expectations worked in the same direction (Lucienne was seen to be his 'préférée'—**162**).

In calm moods, Maurice, like Monique, suggests that all that matters is whether Colette and Lucienne are now happy (**190**), but this is a simplistic criterion, by which Beauvoir herself always set little store, and other factors constitute better pointers. We do, after all, have 'objective' actions and dialogue on the part of the daughters, which offer a sort of crosscheck on different interpretations. There is every sign, for instance, that both daughters are seriously concerned about, and deeply fond of Monique. Moreover, Colette has a favourable view of her upbringing, and Lucienne clearly rejects the suggestion that she left home because Monique was overbearing (**249**). Lucienne's account of the matter—'«je ne suis pas douée pour la vie de famille»' (**248**)—is bound to carry considerable weight in the story, coming as it does right at the end, and is found to be perfectly compatible with Colette's view that 'la vie de famille lui pesait' (**188**).

There is something inherently implausible in Monique's belief that she is to blame for one daughter's faith in love and the other's 'refus de l'amour', so that we are more than inclined to accept Lucienne's claim: '«Tu as toujours eu un sens très exagéré de tes responsabilités»' (250). Her general theory of upbringing offers little consolation to Monique—'Selon elle, ce qui compte dans une enfance, c'est la situation psychanalytique, telle qu'elle existe à l'insu des parents, presque malgré eux' (250), but it again matches Colette's stance: '(Lucienne avait des rapports compliqués avec moi parce qu'elle adorait son père, un Œdipe classique: ça ne prouve rien contre moi)' (188). This whole view has the considerable merit of bringing Maurice back into the centre of the picture. There is absolutely no reason for accepting without debate the assumption that it is the mother who is primarily, or even exclusively responsible for the upbringing of her children and how they develop.

Furthermore, it is vitally important to a measured judgement of the events and characters in 'La Femme rompue' that this point should be generalized to cover marriage as a whole. A signal disadvantage of the angle of Beauvoir's own remarks on the story is that they rather discourage us from attributing to Maurice his fair share of the blame for the breakdown of the marriage and Monique's situation at the end.[2] Even if we have no difficulty in accepting Lucienne's cold, statistical view of marriage (245-6), the fact is that 'La Femme rompue' is not sociological analysis, but a work of fiction in which we are invited to engage with the characters and think in terms of responsibility and blame. We have seen that, beyond any doubt, Monique contributes substantially to her own suffering by her self-deception, but there are obvious dangers in simply assuming that it is clear to all how much Maurice himself is to blame.

Beauvoir talks of the need (supra, p. 52) to 'dépister' Monique, but this should not be allowed to obscure the fact that much of the detective work to be done has to be targeted on Maurice. From the moment when he enters the bedroom in the early hours with a glass of whisky in his hand (130), there is a constant need, for the reader as well as Monique, to decipher Maurice's words and conduct and to interpret what really lies behind them. He has been lying to Monique for eight years or more, and even after his confession about Noëllie he continues to lie to her and deceive her in a variety of ways. It is

---

[2] There is, however, not the slightest justification for Toril Moi's remarkable suggestion that 'to read the text in accordance with Beauvoir's intentions amounts to rejecting the need for any further social or institutional liberation of women' (Moi, p. 72).

not that there is a total lack of explanation for his deceit. But is anyone impressed by his old, familiar justifications that he did not wish to hurt her? that he knew she would explode? that he was ashamed at having lied in the first place? Is anyone tempted to feel sorry for him because he was 'déçu par l'après-guerre'? or because his mother's married life left him with 'une horreur maladive des ruptures'?(**195**) Does he gain our respect by suggesting that Monique has virtually driven him into affairs, and that she has ruined their daughters' lives?

There is actually a considerable problem for the reader, as well as for Monique, in coming to a firm view of Maurice once he has made his initial confession. The stark facts of his conduct thereafter show that he systematically takes more and more away from Monique and gives more and more to Noëllie. It is not surprising that Monique should frequently wonder whether she is being manoeuvred, whether each step has not been premeditated! Yet we ought probably to hesitate before casting Maurice in quite such a cynical light. There is doubtless some truth in his assertions that the matter distresses him too, and there are brief moments when he shows signs of still caring deeply for Monique. Again, Lucienne's 'last word' may be an especially telling one: '«C'est un naïf. Mais pas un salaud»'(**248**).

Such imponderables do nothing to undermine the story, because our main interest inevitably lies in Monique. What the emphasis of Beauvoir's quoted remarks fails to register clearly, however, is the obvious point that we are at least as concerned with Monique's pain and suffering as we are with her 'mauvaise foi'. A major strength of the story, after all, lies in the fact that it records so graphically the horror and the dilemmas of a woman finding herself in Monique's position. Interestingly, this relates more obviously to Beauvoir's account of the origins of the tale than to her detailed description of its content and narrative technique:

> J'avais récemment reçu les confidences de plusieurs femmes d'une quarantaine d'années que leurs maris venaient de quitter pour une autre. [...] leur univers s'écroulait, elles finissaient par ne plus savoir qui elles étaient. D'une autre manière que Laurence elles se débattaient dans l'ignorance et l'idée m'est venue de donner à voir leur nuit. (*TCF*, 175)

It is striking that the notion of self-deception does not figure at all in these particular comments, which suggest a different reading of 'La Femme rompue' from that produced by stress on the self-subverting nature of Monique's diary. This is a potentially simpler reading that primarily involves emphasizing the agonies suffered by Monique as

she reacts to the successive stages of Maurice's affair—agonies that
we may now see as actually compounded by the 'mauvaise foi' of
which she is a victim, and by certain other character flaws. Without
following this reading through in great detail, one can say that
Monique is locked into a series of harrowing dilemmas relating to
the judgements and advice of third parties; the question of what she
can possibly do to help matters; and the stability of her own image of
herself and of Maurice.

The diversity of sources from which Monique seeks help and
advice—women 'friends', Maurice's colleagues, her daughters,
horoscopes, graphologists, a psychiatrist—brings a little colour to
what is otherwise a very bleak and uniform story. But some of these
elements could be taken straight from romantic stories or other items
in popular women's magazines, so that care is needed in interpreting
their significance. Isabelle's exhortation to Monique to be patient and
'compréhensive' (135), for instance, is standard 'agony column'
advice. Yet to stress that the story shows this to be bad advice is to
risk implying that 'La Femme rompue' also fails to question the
assumption that the appropriate goal is indeed to recover Maurice. If
we start from Monique's 'mauvaise foi' and other faults, we are
likely to blame her for following such advice and thereby worsening
her position, whereas a reading of the story centring on Monique's
suffering could emphasize, at this point, the manner in which her
friends and certain other advice-providing forces in society add to
her problems rather than helping her to become an independent
being. In the light of Beauvoir's hostility towards patriarchal
society's pervasive ways of encouraging every woman to think in
terms of catching, hanging on to, or winning back her man, it can be
argued, at the very least, that 'La Femme rompue' attacks this
process less emphatically than might have been expected. In any case,
the central point for present purposes is that, however much
Monique may be responsible for seeking or taking the wrong advice,
or even for ignoring any good advice, her position and state of mind
continue to deteriorate. By the end, by whatever mechanisms, she has
exhausted virtually all possible sources of help and is more alone
than ever.

Such initiatives as Monique herself takes in the course of the story
also fail, and we grow more conscious at every stage that she faces
terrible dilemmas concerning what she can possibly do. Going
through Maurice's pockets, following him, following the pair of
them—these are demeaning as well as ineffectual actions. The
weekend that she wins away with Maurice predictably turns out
badly (159-64), and her attempts to use information that she has

gathered against Noëllie backfire. She can scarcely change her way of life without it looking like a deliberate ploy to win him back (**178-9**). And she is half inclined to cultivate the aspects of her conduct that exasperate him, since it would otherwise seem that everything is too easy for him (**183**). When she tries to insist that Maurice either leave home or break off the affair with Noëllie, she is conscious that this is no more than a kind of play-acting (**185**). In private, her deep sadness prevents her from being active in ways that might improve matters (**203**), and in public she never knows quite how to behave, because of people's knowledge of the situation (**218**).

The extreme confusion of women in Monique's position is such that their whole world crumbles, something that is brought out very powerfully in the diary. It is a violent disorientation that dominates the present, but also extends back over much of the past. Like Madame in 'L'Âge de discrétion', Monique finds herself 'losing' a past that gave meaning and stability to her life: 'Ma vie derrière moi s'est tout entière effondrée, comme dans ces tremblements de terre où le sol se dévore lui-même'(**193**). Either Maurice has changed (and, if so, why? Why has he stopped loving her?), or she has been wrong for more than twenty years and has loved 'un salaud'(**223**). She does not altogether recognize him any more, and her own image of herself becomes blurred. She is too concerned about survival to worry much about how the outside world sees her (**172**), but she cannot understand what Maurice sees when he looks at her (**181**). In short, her present is shattered, her past has crumbled, and her sense of identity is slipping away. Beauvoir acknowledged that she had never written anything more sombre than this story: 'toute la seconde partie n'est qu'un cri d'angoisse et l'effritement final de l'héroïne est plus lugubre qu'une mort'(*TCF,* 178). Monique eventually has a kind of breakdown and bleeds for three weeks, and although there are minute signs that she may be beginning to gather herself together again at the very end, we can scarcely see what the future holds for her.

The author's own remarks on Monique's self-deception can help towards a clearer and deeper understanding of the nature of her character's anguish, ensuring that we look for all of the ways in which Monique contributes to her own tragedy. In the detailed process of exposing her 'mauvaise foi', however, we must beware of assuming that it diminishes her misery in any way. As not infrequently happens with Beauvoir's fiction, we can lay the emphasis on different major elements and thereby draw very different conclusions from her story. For feminist critics in particular, this makes 'La Femme rompue' a peculiarly problematic text. Yet it is difficult to deny, in the end, that the story is extremely successful in making us share the confusion and pain of a betrayed woman, wherever the blame for her situation may lie.

The collection

It is not difficult to see reasons why each story must occupy the position that it does in the order of *La Femme rompue*. 'Monologue' is too disorienting and violent to be placed at the beginning; 'La Femme rompue' too long to be positioned anywhere other than at the end; and the fairly straightforward content of 'L'Âge de discrétion' makes it the ideal tale to open the collection. Again, if we think of the ending of each story, having 'Monologue' as the last would have meant completing the collection on a desperately bleak note, while placing 'L'Âge de discrétion' at the end might have left the reader a little more optimistic than Beauvoir wished and tended to soften the impact made by the plights of the three women as a whole.

For it is clear that the central thrust of the collection is to show us, and have us sympathize with, three women in a state of crisis: 'je me proposais, dans *La Femme rompue*, de peindre les moments critiques de trois existences féminines, la rencontre avec la vieillesse; l'exaspération d'une solitude; la fin brutale d'un amour'.[3] We know that Beauvoir wished to attribute a significant part of the responsibility for their plight to at least two of the women. Long before *Tout compte fait*, she had stressed in her *prière d'insérer*, a kind of author's preface on an accompanying piece of paper which has not been integrated into later editions of *La Femme rompue*, that:

> L'une bute contre une inéluctable fatalité, celle de l'âge. La seconde conjure par un monologue paraphrénique la solitude où l'a jetée son égoïsme éperdu. La femme rompue est la victime stupéfaite de la vie qu'elle s'est choisie [...]. (*PI*, 232)

On the same occasion, however, Beauvoir was also anxious to make clear that there was no question of imparting a moral message about this responsibility, and that her purpose was to convey to the reader the sympathy that she herself felt for such women, even though her own preference was for a different way of tackling life:

---

[3] See her preface to Part I of Anne Ophir's *Regards féminins*, p. 12.

> Je me sens solidaire des femmes qui ont assumé leur vie et qui luttent pour
> la réussir; mais cela ne m'empêche pas—au contraire—de m'intéresser à
> celles qui l'ont plus ou moins manquée et, de manière générale, à cette part
> d'échec qu'il y a dans toute existence. (*PI*, 232)

There is a certain incoherence in these remarks, particularly in
relation to the notions of success, failure, and inevitability, but they
have the merit of discouraging us from laying too much emphasis on
'mauvaise foi' in *La Femme rompue*, and also from oversimplifying
the content of the collection as a whole. The dominant end position
of 'La Femme rompue', and the comments generated by its prior
publication in *Elle*, risk making us think of the collection as focusing
on one fairly simple theme. Yet the volume as a whole is not
centrally about 'la femme abandonnée' (Madame is not deserted by
her husband). Nor does it centre on 'les pièges du dévouement', since
Murielle has been devoted to neither husband nor children.

The more one considers themes and the order of the stories, the
more one comes to discover a certain subtlety in the blend and in the
overall impact of the volume. We might well be tempted to wonder
whether the fury and the near-insanity of Murielle is the extreme
point to which the other two cases (and the thousands of others that
they represent) are tending. Yet, precisely, placing 'Monologue'
between the other two stories 'contains' it in a way that militates
against that gloomiest of conclusions. On the other hand,
'Monologue' has a certain kind of astringent, salutary effect on our
reading (or rereading) of 'L'Âge de discrétion' and 'La Femme
rompue', which might otherwise leave us feeling that not very much
is wrong after all, since when communication between men and
women breaks down it can usually be re-established, and even a
woman whose life has been shattered can begin to pick up the
threads. The three cases in fact balance one another very well,
obliging us to engage without complacency, but also without utter
despair, with the dilemmas of three women who have some common
problems, some very different ones, and quite diverse personal
backgrounds.

It is less clear than Beauvoir implied that all three central figures
have tried to bring time to a halt (Murielle being the problem case);
and although she is right to draw attention to problems of
communication, the differences in the three cases are probably more
significant than any similarities. (Madame actually overcomes some
such difficulties; Murielle deliberately blocks communication, as she
does her telephone bell; and Monique's principal problem is that
Maurice lies to her.) Madame's complacency about communication

which virtually opens the volume (9) is clearly crying out to be undermined, but how many readers will wish, on reflection, to say that she is wrong to believe that we can communicate with at least two or three people? How many writers set out to communicate the point that communication is impossible? In any case, as far as communication between author and reader is concerned, Beauvoir was laying heavy emphasis on this in her comments on literature in 1964.[4] It would be harsh indeed to suggest that she is unsuccessful in her endeavour to communicate the pain of her three heroines, to 'faire entendre ici les voix de trois femmes' (*PI*, 231), to 'donner à voir leur nuit' (*TCF*, 175).

---

[4] In Buin, pp. 73-92. She also made clear her own views on the possibility of communication in everyday life: 'Je ne suis pas de ceux qui croient qu'il n'y a pas dans la vie quotidienne même, une communication' (p. 77).

Conclusion

We have noted that, at least as far as general narrative techniques are concerned, Beauvoir regarded *Les Belles Images* and *La Femme rompue* as works that marked a sharp break with her earlier fiction. A strong feature of much of the critical reaction to the books, moreover, was the rather aggrieved assertion that they were uncharacteristic of the author's writings. And yet it is not at all clear, when one looks at Beauvoir's career after 1968, that these two works ushered in either a new range of preoccupations or a major change of direction in her stylistic concerns as a writer. It is true that they proved, in any case, to be her last two works of fiction; and it is equally true that one of the stories of *La Femme rompue* ('L'Âge de discrétion') deals with the theme of ageing, which she was to take up and develop in her next book, *La Vieillesse* (1970). But the final eighteen years of Beauvoir's life were largely dominated by her relationship with Sartre (increasingly pressing because of his deteriorating state of health) and her militant feminism (which dates from the beginning of the 1970s). The former is reflected in the content of *La Cérémonie des adieux* (1981), which centres exclusively on Sartre, as well in her publication of Sartre's letters in 1983 (*Lettres au Castor et à quelques autres*); and the latter in a stream of published lectures, articles, interviews, book prefaces and open letters—between eighty and a hundred items in all—which constitute a body of writings nearly as remarkable in its way as the monumental *Le Deuxième Sexe.*[1] Yet if there is no particular reason why Beauvoir's subsequent involvement in these two demanding areas of activity should surprise us in the light of *Les Belles Images* and *La Femme rompue,* the books themselves scarcely foreshadow the first, and bear a somewhat problematic relationship to the second.

It may well be rather astonishing for those who know Beauvoir's earlier writings to find how little obvious trace there is of Sartre in these two works. This is not to say that she was no longer working within the broad philosophical framework of Sartre's current ideas in writing them. It is partly to say that there is no male character who bears such strong resemblances to Sartre as, for example, Pierre Labrousse in *L'Invitée* or Dubreuilh in *Les Mandarins.* But it is,

---

[1] Many of those published up to 1977 are listed (and some reproduced) in Francis and Gontier, *Les Écrits de Simone de Beauvoir.* And J.-J. Zéphir systematically draws the content of many of them together in *Le Néo-Féminisme de Simone de Beauvoir.*

above all, to claim that the themes treated no longer have those very close connections with Sartre's specific preoccupations that were such a striking feature of all of Beauvoir's previous novels. If one is inclined to see as the main reason for this the great success of *Le Deuxième Sexe,* which sold extensively in English-speaking countries after the publication of the translation in 1953, this serves only to highlight the interest of the question of how exactly these books relate to Beauvoir's feminism.

Just as she recognized that *Le Deuxième Sexe* itself was not a militant work, although it provided a theoretical base upon which militant feminists could build, so her claim that there is nothing to prevent women from drawing feminist conclusions from *La Femme rompue (TCF,* 179) implies an acknowledgement that it does not make such conclusions obligatory. What indisputably emerges in a general way from both books is the centrality of Beauvoir's concern with the problems of women. But the question of which particular problems are foregrounded in her last two fictional works needs to be treated with some care. For one thing, although each central character is a woman and each is married, with children, other important factors strictly common to all four stories are much less extensive than one might loosely imagine. Each heroine, of course has 'personal' difficulties, but this vague, possibly even vacuous term could not be taken narrowly to mean 'domestic' and would not easily account, for instance, for Laurence's concern for suffering in the world. Moreover, precisely because all four are married women with children (also belonging to the same well-to-do, professional section of the bourgeoisie, being sufficiently rich to have maids, and not to be entirely obliged to work, etc.), we need to recognize that such features as all four stories have in common actually limit their range quite severely. They can deal, at best, only with *certain aspects* of 'la condition féminine' in general.

This is by no means to deny that the unmistakable background to the two books is *Le Deuxième Sexe.* One must suppose that, for readers unfamiliar with the ideas of this text, Beauvoir's last four stories may bring significant revelations concerning male dominance and the secondary position of women in contemporary society. Laurence's hero-worshipping of her father and her heavy dependence upon Jean-Charles will probably prove particularly striking, as will Madame's excessive emotional investment in her son's life and her ultimate dependence upon André. Again, Murielle's pathetic cry for the protection of Tristan is likely to be strongly registered. And, of course, the clearest impression left by 'La Femme rompue' may well be that of Monique's 'dépendance

conjugale qui la laisse dépouillée de tout et de son être même quand
l'amour lui est refusé' (*PI*, 232). These features of the stories,
however, together with the general view of 'love' and men-women
relations upon which they are based, will come as no surprise to
those versed in the argument of *Le Deuxième Sexe*, who are able to
set them into a pre-existing theoretical context. This process
probably does nothing to diminish the power of the stories as
illustrations of the continuing ascendancy of patriarchal values and of
the subtle processes whereby the conditioning of women takes place,
but it does make it easier for such readers to seek those features of
Les Belles Images and *La Femme rompue* that mark them out as
distinctive among Beauvoir's books.

In trying to see the two volumes together, and to look at them
against the background of *Le Deuxième Sexe*, having once noted a
few specific factors common to all of the stories we might think in
terms of parallels, overlap and also of deliberate contrasts within the
same broad framework. After all, while Laurence is in her thirties,
Murielle and Monique are in their forties, and Madame in her
sixties. One works, two do not, and another is retired. One has two
young daughters of school age, another an only son who has left
home, another has two grown-up daughters, and another a daughter
who died and a son living with his father. And so on. It seems that
the variations from story to story under each of these obvious
categories of age, work and child-rearing give as much indication as
do strictly common factors of which particular aspects of women's
situation interest Beauvoir in the two books. The issue of work for
women is one that we would expect to be raised, since *Le Deuxième
Sexe* argued that work constituted the only obviously identifiable
route towards women's independence. 'La Femme rompue',
negatively, is in line with this view, yet the stories as a whole are not
calculated to convey a clear message on the topic. For while
Murielle's lack of a career receives no emphasis at all, and Madame's
past working life is scarcely mentioned, it is difficult to see that
Laurence, the one example of a central figure who does work,
actually benefits from the fact. Again, ageing is a theme in its own
right in 'L'Âge de discrétion', and the loneliness and abandonment of
the heroines in 'Monologue' and 'La Femme rompue' are accentuated
by the fact that they are both in their mid-forties and will therefore
find it difficult to make a new start. Nevertheless, it is already hardly
the same sense of 'ageing' that is involved, and, in any case, one can
hardly talk of ageing as such in connection with Laurence, even if
she is very conscious that she married too young and, rightly or

wrongly, now considers it too late to change her life. Once more, then, it is a spectrum of factors that Beauvoir is treating, rather than one particular situation. Whether or not as a consequence of this fact, it appears that, in relation to *Le Deuxième Sexe,* the two books add nothing of substance to the theory of women's ageing or to the subject of women and work, although it is worth reiterating the point that, as stories, they might legitimately be expected to serve other purposes.

The matter of child-rearing or upbringing in general, however, is so prominent in these stories as a whole that it deserves especially careful consideration. As his existential biographies and his autobiography show, Sartre too was preoccupied with the importance of childhood, but there are a number of quite distinctive features to Beauvoir's treatment of the issue of upbringing in *Les Belles Images* and *La Femme rompue.* Firstly, of course, she places almost all of the emphasis upon the mother's role, and it needs to be admitted that this is by no means an altogether satisfactory aspect of the texts. It is not that there is no recognition at all of the father's role: for three of the four heroines the love of, and love for, their father has been vital to their own formation; each of the four has (or, in Murielle's case, has had) a husband who has exercised some direct influence upon the children; and the various references to 'la situation psychanalytique' in any given family imply that the father's presence may be as crucial as the mother's. Nevertheless, almost all of the detailed material in the books is—doubtless because Beauvoir saw this as reflecting current reality[2]—in line with the traditional view that it is first and foremost the mother who consciously devotes time to, and commits herself to, the rearing of the children, with the father seeking to enact only a much more limited, usually intellectual role.

The heart of the problem, on the literary level, lies in the fact that in all cases narration is exclusively from the woman's point of view. (Beauvoir herself admitted that, at least in *La Femme rompue,* 'je n'ai guère cherché à élucider le rôle des hommes'.)[3] In spite of the point that 'Monologue', 'La Femme rompue', and even to a degree 'L'Âge de discrétion', are cautionary tales, warning against the unreliability of certain women's testimony, the very form of each of the four stories prevents us from ever seeing things through the

---

[2] 'Chez nous, l'enfant naît par hasard, la mère l'élève sans secours, les mœurs exigent qu'elle en assume presque exclusivement la charge: la coopération du père est secondaire même si elle travaille et gagne autant que lui' (Beauvoir, 'La Condition féminine', p. 123).

[3] In Ophir, p. 12. Beauvoir's idea that a 'vérité partielle' constitutes a mystification only if it is taken as the whole truth (in Buin, p. 80) could be either a justification or a timely warning in this connection.

father's eyes, and therefore from making a balanced judgement on the father's contribution to the upbringing process. (An observation made by one of Monique's friends in 'La Femme rompue' about love relationships— '«Ces histoires de rupture, racontées par la femme, on n'y comprend jamais rien»' [197]—is equally applicable to child-rearing). Little of the material considered under the theme of 'upbringing' would have to be left aside if one focused specifically on the theme of 'motherhood'. For there are other major gaps or deficiencies in the treatment of upbringing as such in the stories. Clearly the problems of being a male offspring cannot possibly be directly examined, any more than can a boy's relations with siblings (although it is less clear why sister-to-sister relations should be touched on only in the most superficial fashion). And, as was implicit in earlier remarks, we are given no idea of what an upbringing actually dominated by the father might amount to. It might be argued that there is no reason why Beauvoir should not deal with the theme of motherhood rather than upbringing as such, but in these stories there are enough acknowledgements of the importance of the father's role in the latter process to leave such a choice looking an oddly uncomfortable one.

Nevertheless, the characteristic emphasis in the two books actually complicates the issue of child-rearing in one particular way, by giving prominence to the point that any mother is herself the product of a particular upbringing (the same is of course true of fathers, but again this receives scant attention). The implications of this simple fact are traced with persistence and skill by Beauvoir, who uses to good effect the recognition that a mother may, consciously or unconsciously, bring up her children in the very way that she herself was raised; or may resolutely react against her own mother's methods. *Les Belles Images,* moreover, shows awareness of the further truism that the influence of the particular upbringing of every mother's mother has similarly to be taken into account. We are obviously no more in the realm of new theoretical insights here than we were in the case of ageing or women's careers, and the belief upon which the books appear to be based, that an individual is somehow marked for life by her childhood, is left worryingly vague.[4] But the stories do undoubtedly contain powerful and memorable fictional embodiments of a narrow range of particular aspects of upbringing, and feature images, incidents and dilemmas of

---

[4] Scrutiny of Beauvoir's most detailed pronouncements on the subject, in her interviews with Jeanson and in *Tout compte fait,* confirms that her views on the importance remained theoretically imprecise, in their complete failure to elucidate the actual mechanism of 'conditioning' or 'programming'.

the sort that Beauvoir believed would involve a reader more than theoretical pronouncements.

In the light of her consistent belief that a good work of fiction can never be reduced to a set of philosophical assertions, we should not be altogether surprised to find that the treatment of upbringing here does not simply amount to saying—as some would doubtless want the stories to say—that it is merely social conditioning. Indeed, this general belief is not one that emerges with any clarity at all from the particular cases portrayed in these stories. Two of the four heroines (Laurence and Madame) are set on bringing up their children to oppose at least certain specific values instantiated in the society around them, and a third (Murielle) claims to have done exactly the same thing. The fourth (Monique) may have left her daughters to develop freely, as she herself believes, or may have rather oppressed them, but in either case she has produced two very different results: one daughter who appears to be conforming to social role models, and another who has definitely rejected them. An important observation following from this is that, although in a general way the stories reflect a society in which women are conditioned to think of themselves as wives and mothers rather than independent human beings, it is very doubtful whether this particular point could be considered as a central feature of any of them.

More generally, one can say that the role of society in these books is a somewhat less influential one than many of Beauvoir's later sociopolitical pronouncements might have led us to expect. In spite of one of her claims about *La Femme rompue,* that in this collection she was expressing 'l'ensemble de la société d'aujourd'hui, telle qu'elle se découvre à nous, à partir de notre condition de femme',[5] only in *Les Belles Images* is contemporary society itself a focus of attention. As we saw, 'L'Âge de discrétion' does no more than make a few rather half-hearted references to social and political issues. In 'Monologue' the admittedly frequent allusions to the iniquities of the twentieth century are fragmentary and idiosyncratic; if true, they are 'accidentally' true, in that Murielle's whole view is distorted and pathological. And the presence of society as such in 'La Femme rompue' is shadowy in the extreme; the personal drama almost takes place within the same kind of self-contained 'cercle magique' that encloses the triangle of characters in *L'Invitée.* This may be part of the significance of the fact that we see Monique take on another 'social case', the waif Marguerite, at the beginning of the story, but gradually let it slip away as her personal problems come to dominate.

---

[5] In Ophir, p. 12.

None of this is to suggest that society as a backcloth, or even a setting, has no importance at all in the stories of *La Femme rompue.* Nor is it to deny that, as that society comes to the fore from time to time, it is discernibly the same technocratic, consumer society as in *Les Belles Images.* An interesting little task for the reader is to spot the moments at which characters and social situations that might have been taken straight from the novel appear in the stories of the collection (in 'L'Âge de discrétion', Irène and her parents, and the job that they find for Philippe; in 'Monologue', the people in the flats around Murielle, and at least some of the circles in which she has mixed, including Tristan's; in 'La Femme rompue', Noëllie and her crowd, the world into which Maurice is increasingly drawn). But these elements cannot be said to be, or even come near, the centre of attention in *La Femme rompue,* whereas 'la société technocratique' is unquestionably a theme in its own right in *Les Belles Images.*

We might well still wish to argue that, since we are dealing with four separate stories, one of the limitations of the two books taken together is that they draw their characters and situations from an extremely narrow range. The questions that can be asked about society, about upbringing, about women are, as we have already begun to see, restricted by the very lack of variety in social settings and narrative viewpoints. In general terms, however, this might be a difficult criticism to sustain, since there are no obvious guidelines to tell us what can legitimately be asked of a writer in the space of four stories. Yet the matter is a somewhat sensitive one in Beauvoir's case, if only because of the feminist expectations generated by *Le Deuxième Sexe.* She was surely right to believe that she was under no obligation to depict feminist heroines or examples to be followed in her fiction (*TCF,* 179). To say that there are no positive gender models in the two books is simply to express in another form the point already made: that the women in the stories are shown as being in more or less the state of dependence upon men that so concerned Beauvoir in *Le Deuxième Sexe.* She considered the describing of such dependency in works of fiction to be perfectly consistent with feminism. We know, moreover, that in the 1960s she became increasingly preoccupied by the lack of progress made since 1949 in women's struggle for emancipation. As far as the efficacity of particular feminist activities is concerned, however, in the end it is for the individual reader to judge whether Beauvoir actually served the feminist cause well in depicting, in four stories, four bourgeois women experiencing serious difficulties in connection with their marriages and their children.

For those who believe she did, there are further questions to answer concerning the manner in which she did so. Some would presumably wish she had portrayed her four protagonists entirely as victims of patriarchal society, but any careful reader of *Le Deuxième Sexe* will know that this was never remotely likely. One of the epigraphs to the second volume of that book (taken from Sartre) sums up the point neatly: 'À moitié victimes, à moitié complices, comme tout le monde'. Hence the emphasis on Laurence's complicity with the society to which she belongs, including its role models; and on the 'mauvaise foi' of the narrators of each of the stories in *La Femme rompue*. Such emphasis involves the reader's close, line by line participation, as we have noted. But we can see now that, at a more general level, it also requires the reader to fit what are not obviously feminist pieces into what is broadly a feminist pattern. For example, even the debilitating 'dépendance conjugale' of Monique already referred to (*supra,* pp. 68-69) has to be seen as a self-inflicted ill: 'La femme rompue est la victime stupéfaite de la vie qu'elle s'est choisie [...]' (*PI,* 232). Once more, some may judge that it was an unwise, counterproductive move for a feminist to portray, over four stories, only women in collusion with society, self-deceived women. On the other hand, a major reason for ultimately disagreeing with such a judgement is that Beauvoir is giving prominence to those aspects of women's condition over which they have direct control, aspects which they themselves, individually rather than collectively, can change.

The particular angle from which Beauvoir approaches her subject in these two books and the technical differences from her previous novels that this implies can indeed be regarded as something of a renewal for her within the realm of fiction, a new departure that means involving her readers more actively in the reading process ('Demander au public de lire entre les lignes, c'est dangereux. J'ai réitéré cependant'—*TCF,* 175). It is fairly clear that both the tone and the precise moral/political preoccupations of, say, *Le Sang des autres, Tous les hommes sont mortels,* or *Les Mandarins* would have been out of place in fiction produced in the mid-1960s. A strong, prescriptive emphasis on personal freedom, with all that it implies, would have struck an odd chord, both for readers and for the author herself, who was increasingly conscious of the weight of upbringing and of direct and indirect social pressures that falls upon individual women. But Beauvoir still stopped short of the deterministic position of regarding women as no more than passive victims, regarding her characters as partly responsible for their fate, and wishing her readers themselves to uncover their complicity and self-deception.

The reception of the two books makes it perfectly plain, however, that she is often unsuccessful in this last intention. There is reason for suggesting that she might have thought more carefully about her actual readership.[6] In any case, one can say that the participation on the part of the reader here is more complex than in Beauvoir's earlier fiction. One does not have to be in the same position as her protagonists to appreciate their dilemmas; nor does one have to be of the same sex in order to share many of their feelings. Laurence, locked into a society that she disapproves of; Madame, aware of the ageing process forced upon her; Murielle, lonely, paranoid and ostracized in indistinguishable proportions; Monique, bewildered by an irreparable loss, which she may or may not have brought upon herself—these are figures that readers of different sexes and from very different situations, will recognize, relate to, and perhaps find somewhere in themselves. But, equally, the more carefully they read, and reread the texts, the more likely they are, on the whole, to begin to detach themselves from the protagonists, to see their dilemmas (and thereby, perhaps, their own) in a rather different perspective: 'moi lecteur, ce qui m'importe c'est d'être fasciné par un monde singulier qui se recoupe avec le mien et pourtant qui est autre'.[7] Even if this is not an especially unusual literary phenomenon, it is one particularly well suited to conveying the ambiguity of women's position in relation to patriarchal society ('à moitié victimes, à moitié complices'), and perhaps of everyone's position in relation to contemporary western society ('comme tout le monde').

In the second major phase of the development of their thought, both Sartre and Beauvoir came to accept the importance of the 'conditioning' that we all experience in childhood, but they did not renounce entirely the idea of individual freedom so prominent in their earlier existentialist period: 'je ne dirai pas que tout est donné, puisque je crois qu'il y aura ensuite une constante reprise de l'existence et de soi-même'.[8] More than this, they believed that in exercising our freedom in relation to our beginnings, we make choices that take on a reality of their own and, in their turn, make further demands upon us. This dialectical process is caught particularly well in *Les Belles Images* and *La Femme rompue,* where the main characters are re-evaluating, or trying to come to terms

---

[6] She seems to acknowledge in *Tout compte fait* (p. 173) that she had not fully considered the nature of her reading public. And Elizabeth Fallaize (1990) treats this question in an interesting way with respect to the serialization of 'La Femme rompue' in *Elle.*

[7] In Buin, p. 81.

[8] In Jeanson, p. 252.

with, choices that they made earlier on the basis of their upbringing, and which have had consequences that are now pressing in upon them. And the same process, fascinatingly, is mirrored in the way in which we, as readers, are also called upon to turn back upon ourselves, to re-evaluate earlier interpretations of the characters. In spite of their limitations, Beauvoir's last two works of fiction can claim to set up distinctive kinds of dialogue between reader and character, and thereby to tackle a certain range of themes in a way very different from that followed in her earlier fiction, but one no less forceful and impressive in its own right. Although one might wish to consider substituting 'femme' for 'homme', the two books measure up quite well to the claim that Beauvoir made about literature in 1964:

> Sauvegarder contre les technocraties et contre les bureaucraties ce qu'il y a d'humain dans l'homme, livrer le monde dans sa dimension humaine, c'est-à-dire en tant qu'il se dévoile à des individus à la fois liés entre eux et séparés, je crois que c'est la tâche de la littérature et ce qui la rend irremplaçable. (Buin, p. 92)

Postscript

'Malentendu à Moscou'

In June 1992, a French academic journal printed a previously unpublished story of some 21,000 words by Beauvoir, 'Malentendu à Moscou', of which there is no mention either in her memoirs or in biographies.[1] The editor suggests that it was due to be included in *La Femme rompue*, and, since whole textual sequences from it have been simply transferred into 'L'Âge de discrétion', one must consider the latter as having, in some sense, *replaced* 'Malentendu à Moscou' in the collection. But whatever Beauvoir's reasons may have been for setting her Moscow story aside, it will henceforth have a permanent place in the body of her published fiction, and both its similarities with the tales actually published in the 1960s and its differences from these are of particular interest. The reader is likely to notice immediately three distinctive features. Firstly, there is a major difference in Beauvoir's broad narrative strategy. Secondly, while the elderly married couple André and Nicole clearly correspond quite closely to the couple in 'L'Âge de discrétion', Nicole's stepdaughter Macha has no counterpart in the latter story. Thirdly, 'Malentendu à Moscou' includes a good deal of detail and comment on the state of the Soviet Union in 1966, giving it a more significant social and political content than can be ascribed to any of the stories in *La Femme rompue* and making it in some measure complementary to the treatment of Western society in *Les Belles Images*.[2]

Beauvoir's main narrative principle concerning focalization continues to be followed in 'Malentendu à Moscou', but she reverts to the technique used in two earlier novels, whereby the focus of the narration alternates regularly between one male and one female character. (There are no separate chapters, but most of the changes of focaliser are clearly marked by gaps in the text, with twelve sections centring on Nicole and twelve on André.)[3] Unlike her other

---

[1] *Roman 20-50. Revue d'étude du roman du XXe siècle*, no. 13. Subsequent bracketed page references are to this number of the journal.

[2] I shall not dwell on this here. Some relevant points are brought out in my 'Commitment, Re-Commitment and Puzzlement: Aspects of the Cold War in the Fiction of Simone de Beauvoir'.

[3] There is thus a need for some modification of any suggestion that this pattern was deliberately supplanted, in Beauvoir's fiction, by the strategy of a single woman focalizer, since the story was written after *Les Belles Images*.

stories of the same period, therefore, it presents certain themes like ageing not from one point of view, but from two; not just from the woman's standpoint, but also from the man's. The importance of this is considerable. We see directly, for instance, that Nicole's claim that André is not conscious of ageing is simply mistaken, since most of the sections focused on André demonstrate some aspect or other of his awareness of his age. Furthermore, because he is shown as having a similar illusion about Nicole, the reader's reaction at the end, when they come to see and articulate their mistakes, is one of recognition rather than discovery. The more specific 'malentendu' between them nearly two thirds of the way through the story crystallises certain problems of communication, which are themselves bound up with ageing, but at this point giving access to the mentality of both partners presents Beauvoir with a problem. The reason why she has the crucial incident happen when they are both tired and rather drunk (so that neither has an entirely reliable recollection of exactly what took place) is that she is determined to make 'Malentendu à Moscou' a story in which husband and wife are equally blameworthy for the misunderstandings and disagreements that occur between them. In general, the eventual reconciliation between the couple is likely to carry more weight than in 'L'Âge de discrétion', by virtue of the reader's capacity see the viewpoint of both parties, and near the end Beauvoir is able to use particular technical devices to reinforce the effect. The huge predominance of dialogue as such in the last three pages of the text is one factor, but it is also noticeable that three of the final four changes of viewpoint are *not* marked by a gap in the text. Indeed, they are not instantly detectable, and twice the transitional sentences could be taken as expressing the viewpoint of either Nicole or André (**184**; **185**). This is an intriguing way of indicating that both partners are at the same point in their relationship, struggling to make the initial reconciliation into the basis for a permanently improved mutual understanding.

There are other interesting elements or dimensions to 'Malentendu à Moscou' that are missing from 'L'Âge de discrétion': one might almost say *excised* from it. For instance, the references to Nicole's development and thinking in relation to her womanhood build up an unusually detailed picture. She aggressively resisted male superiority when she was young, but apparently became reconciled to her gender when she met André (**183-4**). However, the rather conventional and troublefree course of their early relationship did not prevent the occurrence of certain problems in their later married life, and we learn through André that Nicole gave up sex at a particular moment some years before the trip to Moscow (**144**); it is even suggested that she may, after all, have never *quite* accepted her womanhood (**163**). The significance of this admission is increased by the fact that we come closer in 'Malentendu à Moscou' than in any of Beauvoir's other novels or stories to having a chronologically complete, if sketchy, outline of the whole sexual life of a woman character, from adolescence to old age. Her feminist beginnings—she is surely the only major woman character in Beauvoir's fiction to have been a militant feminist—make her case a special one, yet she may ultimately be as much the victim of a world of male dominance as her counterparts, having eventually been devoured by 'son mari, son fils, son foyer' (**164**). She is not the positive heroine that some feminists look for in Beauvoir's stories, but it is vital to recognise that, unlike characters such as Murielle and Monique in *La Femme rompue*, she readily accepts some of the responsibility for all that has and has not happened to her (**169**).

An aspect of 'Malentendu à Moscou' deserving particular attention is the fascinating web of relationships that encompasses not only Nicole herself, André and their son Philippe, but also Nicole's stepdaughter Macha. Although it is not foregrounded in the same way, Nicole's bond with her son has more in common with its equivalent in 'L'Âge de discrétion' than is immediately apparent, but the complexity and depth of the forces and family tensions involved are greatly accentuated by the presence in the story of Macha. Especially as it is stressed that Nicole is very well-disposed towards her stepdaughter, much of the focus and emphasis falls upon André's own relationship with an adult daughter who set out to get to know him only some six years earlier. His reactions are seen to have had some implications for his relations with Nicole, for, although there appears to be nothing more unhealthy about his affection for Macha than there is in Nicole's strong attachment to Philippe, the suggestion is that the elderly couple may both—at different times—have diverted some of the intensity of their earlier love into relations with their offspring. The fact that they are now passing through this stage provides a rather more resonant context in which to show them hesitantly turning back to each other than the one that prevails at the end of 'L'Âge de discrétion'.

Nevertheless, it is still instructive to ask whether the 'extra' elements in 'Malentendu à Moscou' might in some way have detracted from the power and focus of *La Femme rompue*. While Beauvoir gives the collection as published a strong unity by writing each of the stories only from the viewpoint of the central woman figure, she also encourages the reader to explore different degrees and forms of self-deception in women over-dependent upon men. It is clear that, had 'Malentendu à Moscou' taken the place of 'L'Âge de discrétion', further processes of comparison and contrast would have been required of the reader, and the issue of blame for problems in marital relationships would not have been seen in quite the same perspective. For better or worse, this might have left *La Femme rompue* aligned in a slightly more obvious way with Beauvoir's explicit argument in the conclusion of *Le Deuxième Sexe* that men and women bear more or less equal responsibility for the current status of women in society.

Although, as we noted from the first, *La Femme rompue* cannot sensibly be said to be autobiographical in nature, those determined to locate Beauvoir's personal life behind her books will be interested in the speculation that she replaced 'Malentendu à Moscou' in the collection because it constituted too obvious a transposition of her concern about Sartre's liaison with their female Russian interpreter, Lena Zonina. On the other hand, if it comes to seem more likely that the principal reason for the replacement was a series of developments in the Soviet Union in 1966-1967 which caused severe disillusionment,[4] then this might suggest that broader sociopolitical questions of the kind raised in *Les Belles Images* were somewhat more important to Beauvoir than is often assumed. In the meantime, the multidimensional nature of 'Malentendu à Moscou', together with certain unique psychological elements that it contains, make for a story that considerably enriches the range of Beauvoir's later fiction. It will undoubtedly yield further points of interest, as well as other links, as it is subjected to more detailed analysis.

---

[4] I have speculated briefly about both of these possibilities in my article, 'Malentendu à Moscou', which also offers a general analysis of the story.

Select Bibliography

Place of publication of books written in French is Paris, and of books written in English, London, unless otherwise stated.

(a) Relevant works by Beauvoir

Fiction

L'Invitée. Gallimard, 1943.

Le Sang des autres. Gallimard, 1945.

Tous les hommes sont mortels. Gallimard, 1946.

Les Mandarins. Gallimard, 1954.

Les Belles Images. Gallimard, 1966.
Edition referred to: 'Folio'.

La Femme rompue. Gallimard, 1968.
Edition referred to: 'Folio'.

Quand prime le spirituel. Gallimard, 1979.

'Malentendu à Moscou',
Roman 20-50. Revue d'étude du roman du XXe siècle
(Université de Lille III), 13 (juin 1992), 137-88.

Autobiographical Texts

Mémoires d'une jeune fille rangée. Gallimard, 1958.

La Force de l'âge. Gallimard, 1960.

La Force des choses. Gallimard, 1963.

Une mort très douce. Gallimard, 1964.

Tout compte fait (TCF). Gallimard, 1972.
Edition referred to: 'Folio'.

Essays

Le Deuxième Sexe. Gallimard, 1949 (2 vols.).
Edition referred to: 'Folio' (2 vols.).

La Vieillesse. Gallimard, 1970.

Feminism and Literary Theory

'Littérature et Métaphysique', in Beauvoir, *L'Existentialisme et la sagesse des nations* (Nagel, 1948), pp. 89-107.

'La Condition féminine', *La Nef*, no.5 (janv.-mars 1961), 121-7.
Reprinted in Francis and Gontier (1979), 401-9.

Lecture on literature (1964) in Buin, Y. (ed.), *Que peut la littérature?* (U.G.E., collection 'L'Inédit, 10/18', 1965), pp. 73-92.

Interview with Madeleine Gobeil (1964) in *Cité Libre,* août-septembre 1964. Extracts reprinted in Julienne-Caffié, 211-18.

Two interviews with Francis Jeanson (1965) in Jeanson, 250-98.

Interview with Jacqueline Piatier (1966) in *Le Monde,* 23 décembre 1966. Reprinted in Stefanson, pp. 55-61.

'Situation de la femme d'aujourd'hui', lecture given in Japan (1966), in Francis and Gontier (1979), pp. 422-38.

(b) Biography and bibliography

Bair, D., *Simone de Beauvoir: A Biography.* Jonathan Cape, 1990.

Bennett, J. and Hochmann, G., *Simone de Beauvoir. An Annotated Bibliography.* Garland, 1988.

Francis, C. and Gontier, F., *Les Écrits de Simone de Beauvoir.* Gallimard, 1979.

Francis, C. and Gontier, F., *Simone de Beauvoir.* Perrin, 1985.

(c) Selected critical works and articles

Chapsal, M., 'Une belle mécanique', *Quinzaine littéraire,* 18 (15-31 décembre 1966).

Evans, M., *Simone de Beauvoir: A Feminist Mandarin.* Tavistock, 1985.

Fallaize, E., *The Novels of Simone de Beauvoir.* Routledge, 1988.

————, 'Resisting romance: Simone de Beauvoir, "The Woman Destroyed" and the romance script', in Atack, M. and Powrie, P. (eds.), *Contemporary French Fiction by Women: Feminist Perspectives* (Manchester University Press, 1990), pp. 15-25.

Heath, J., *Simone de Beauvoir.* Hemel Hempstead: Harvester Wheatsheaf, 1989.

Jeanson, F., *Simone de Beauvoir ou l'entreprise de vivre.* Seuil, 1966.

Julienne-Caffié, S., *Simone de Beauvoir.* Gallimard, 1966.

Keefe, T., 'Marriage in the later fiction of Camus and Simone de Beauvoir', *Orbis Litterarum,* 33 (1978), 69-86.

————, 'Psychiatry in the post-war fiction of Simone de Beauvoir', *Literature and Psychology,* XXIX (1979), 300-14.

————, *Simone de Beauvoir. A Study of Her Writings.* Harrap, 1983.

————, 'Malentendu à Moscou', *Simone de Beauvoir Studies,* 11 (1994), 30-41.

————, 'Commitment, re-commitment and puzzlement: aspects of the Cold War in the fiction of Simone de Beauvoir', *French Cultural Studies,* VIII (1997), 127-36.

————, *Simone de Beauvoir.* Macmillan, 'Modern Novelists', 1998.

Lasocki, A.-M., *Simone de Beauvoir ou l'entreprise d'écrire.* The Hague: Martinus Nijhoff, 1971.

Moi, T., 'Intentions and effects: rhetoric and identification in Simone
    de Beauvoir's "The Woman Destroyed"', in her *Feminist
    Theory and Simone de Beauvoir* (Oxford: Basil Blackwell,
    1990), pp. 61-93.

Moubachir, C., *Simone de Beauvoir ou le souci de différence*.
    Seghers, 1972.

Okely, J., *Simone de Beauvoir*. Virago, 1986.

Ophir, A., *Regards féminins*. Denoël/Gonthier, 1976.

Pagès, I., 'Beauvoir's *Les Belles Images*: "desubstantification" of
    reality through a narrative', *Forum for Modern Language
    Studies*, XI (1975), 133-41.

Simon, P.-H., '*Les Belles Images* de Simone de Beauvoir', *Le
    Monde*, 25 janvier 1967. Reprinted in Stefanson, pp. 65-69.

Stefanson, B. (ed.), *Simone de Beauvoir: 'Les Belles Images'*.
    Heinemann Educational, 1980.

Zéphir, J.-J., *Le Néo-féminisme de Simone de Beauvoir*. Denoël/
    Gonthier, 1982.

———

The following numbers of *Simone de Beauvoir Studies* all contain
articles on *Les Belles Images* and/or *La Femme rompue*: 4 (1987);
5 (1988); 6 (1989); 8 (1991); 9 (1992); 10 (1993); 11 (1994).